THE POWERS OF ANCIENT
AND
SACRED PLACES

Paul Devereux

DAILY GRAIL PUBLISHING

CONTENTS

AUTHOR'S PREFACE

In 1990, I wrote a book called *Places of Power,* that was, essentially, an account up to that point of something called the "Dragon Project" – founded in order to explore rumours about the supposed powers and properties of some ancient, especially prehistoric, 'sacred' places and monuments. In this present volume I will draw on selected, updated and recontextualised sections of material from that book where they are still germane, and also elements from other of my writings where relevant, in addition to further research and investigation by myself and many others – much water has passed beneath the metaphorical bridge in the past three decades. So much so, that this book presents a whole new, updated and extended scope and assessment of the multifarious powers of sacred places, containing avenues of investigation undreamt of back when *Places of Power* was being written.

The scope of this present work covers some aspects of my personal involvement over decades, thus while attempting to maintain a degree of rigour I have also not shied away from interjecting first-person informal elements from time to time where I feel it helps elucidate matters.

I should point out that this book will tell of some of the remarkableness, strangeness and mystery of the *human* story in relation to ancient monumental and venerated sites, so there will be no claims about ancient aliens, lost Atlanteans and similar sensational and misleading populist 'ancient mysteries' tropes in this book. Of course, some people, especially those in the academic mainstream, will find things here challenging and controversial, but hopefully they can temporarily park any instinctive prejudices and see this work as a reasonably intelligent and honest effort from which they can hopefully glean at least a few points of interest concerning the nature of some ancient sites. We have not yet read the whole book of nature, nor the full record of human ways of thinking.

Paul Devereux
Cotswolds, England
June, 2020

Prologue

THE DRAGON PROJECT

The Dragon Project (website: www.dragonprojecttrust.org) was founded in 1977 (a Trust from 1988), to explore rumours about the power and properties of ancient, especially prehistoric, 'sacred' places and monuments. The objective of the Trust is to publish and otherwise promulgate its findings in keeping with it being an educational charity. It is an independent entity, indeed, a 'shoestring' pilot effort, that relies on goodwill, volunteerism, and, where forthcoming, public donations and other funding from grant-making bodies in order to conduct its investigations. Some work is even funded directly out of the pockets of DPT members. Its areas of interest include the study of physical, measurable energies at sites; an exploration of human psycho-physical reactions and interactions at sites, and multi-sensory properties of sites, especially acoustical properties (archaeoacoustics).

Some of these areas are considered "fringe", others, such as archaeoacoustics, not so much. The Dragon Project Trust (DPT) itself operates strictly in a neutral capacity to see what basis if any lies behind various claims, and where there seems to be such a basis, to explore further as its limited resources allow. It is not an exponent of New Age (or other) belief systems.

The genesis of the Project was in a series of meetings I had convened in the late 1970s with a small group of people covering a range of subject areas to see if there was sufficient interest in forming such a project. There was. But we had scant idea of where and how to start such a daunting and, frankly, over-ambitious project. Progress was, and remains, sporadic and slow due to lack of resources in terms of funding and people's time, with a shifting cast of volunteers. But, as we have often said on the Project to bolster ourselves, mainstream archaeology wouldn't touch a subject like the 'powers of ancient places' with a bargepole, perhaps understandably, so that whatever little we could achieve or clarify would be better than nothing at all.

EARLY DAYS

In the first months, appeals were made for expertise and funds. Modest sums were donated from the public (largely readers of *The Ley Hunter* magazine) and electronic components for initial instrumentation were obtained, letterheads printed, and field equipment such as tents purchased. Useful funding was provided by a brave grant from the Threshold Foundation UK, and a few hundred additional pounds were donated by the British Society of Dowsers. (In much more recent years a modest bequest by Patrick Horsbrugh has been most welcome.) It was not a lot, but it allowed the Project to proceed in its own tentative way, and for a coordinating office to be set up.

Through the good offices of author, IT expert and dowser Tom Graves, permission was obtained from the owner of the Rollright stone circle, the late Pauline Flick, to use the site as the Project's main field base. The Rollright Stones complex, near Oxford, was a particularly suitable choice, as the site has easy access, and it has a rich body of folklore attached to it (detailed later). Moreover, in the fields around the circle were other, associated, megalithic sites: the now lone monolith known as the King Stone lies about a hundred metres to the north of the stone circle,

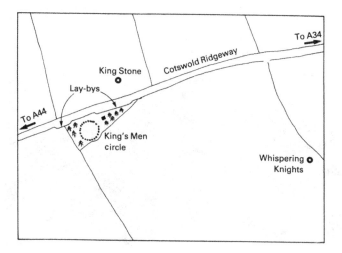

Figure 1. Plan of the core Rollright Stones complex, showing the layout
of the main extant sites relative to one another. The country road running
through the complex marks the course of an ancient ridgeway.

which is called 'The King's Men', and a collapsed portal dolmen
known as the 'Whispering Knights' is about 400 metres (1,300ft)
away in an adjacent field to the south-east and is probably older
than the other components of the Rollright Stones complex. In
recent years, aerial survey has revealed that the Stones were part
of a whole complex of standing stones, earthworks and ancient
trackways – a veritable prehistoric crossroads.

The overarching legend about the Rollright Stones is that
a king was marching across country followed by his men with
the knights bringing up the rear. But there are numerous other
folklore themes attached to the sites; one, belonging to the King's
Men circle stated that the stones could not be counted, and it
is true that the few ground plans of the site had shown varying
numbers of stones. This would have probably been due to local
farmers clearing large rocks from their fields and dumping them
at the site, and also there had been a partial reconstruction of the

Figure 2. The northern half of the King's Men stone circle, Rollright.

circle in the late 19th Century. So, in October 1978, archaeologist John Barnatt produced a fresh survey of the Rollright circle for the Project (Figure 3), in which he probed the bases of the stones so that we would have a good idea of which ones in the ring were most likely to be original.

As the fieldwork commenced, the Project's geological consultant, Paul McCartney, began to study a claim made by an author, the late John Michell in 1969, that megalithic sites were located close to significant or moderately significant, geological faulting. Faults are cracks or fissures in the earth's crust, and often create localized regions of disturbed electromagnetic energy within the landscape. They are also typical features in the kind of terrain that seems to attract unusual light phenomena, as we will learn later. McCartney's research was able to confirm Michell's informal observation at least as far as stone circles are concerned. And Rollright fitted the pattern: the circle is indeed only a field away from an isolated local fault – the Rollright Fault, no less.

Over the years, many sites other than Rollright have been visited by Dragon Project personnel – even as far-flung as the King's Chamber in Egypt's Great Pyramid – but the Oxfordshire circle remained the main reference headquarters for the Project through its earlier years.

Core personnel other than myself on the Dragon Project included American anthropologist, John Steele, and Roy Cooper, a now-retired surveyor then attached to Oxford University, and born and bred in the county. He became the local anchorman at Rollright and shouldered a great deal of the Project's local monitoring work. And we were also joined by Rodney Hale, a professional electronics engineer with his own electronics design company. Around the core team, many experts and general helpers came and went over subsequent months and years.

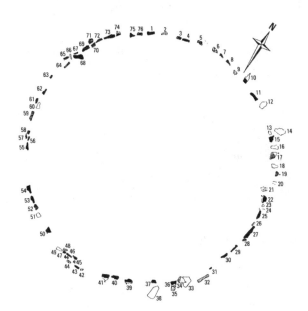

Figure 3. John Barnatt's 1978 survey of the King's Men stone circle, Rollright. The inked-in stones are those most likely to have been original, and those in tone are less certainly original. (© John Barnatt)

Figure 4. An old print showing a view from the Whispering Knights towards the King's Men in the distance.

Subsequent to the Dragon Project's energy investigations among the Rollright Stones, archaeologist George Lambrick and his team conducted a variety of archaeological investigations at the complex (Lambrick 1983).

WHERE TO START?

Although the range of investigations undertaken by the Project has expanded into other areas of interest in recent times, as we shall see, its initial concern was to take a closer look at popular notions concerning anomalous physical 'energies' at ancient sites. This was a difficult proposition because people have made the wildest speculations regarding energy effects at prehistoric sites, and it was difficult to sort the wheat from the chaff in such accounts. When the Dragon Project was formed, it was simply popularly *assumed* that strange energies existed at these places. The whole subject was confused, with statements of belief, pet theories, and speculation intermingling with purported actual experiences. The Project wanted to see what was actually *known*, and to figure out which reported effects might indicate the presence of some basic and measurable physical energy behaviour onto which more fantastical ideas may have been laminated. But the potential range such physical monitoring could involve was intimidating, and clearly beyond the capacity of a small, volunteer outfit. After all, the detailed study of any one aspect of the energy environment could swallow up the resources of whole university departments. But it was also realised that we were in virgin research territory, and that *anything* fresh we might manage to find out would be more than was currently known.

In order to make best use of our inevitably limited research resources it was clear that a way to go about it was to target what seemed to be fairly reliable anecdotal material regarding energy effects at sites and to see what lines of enquiry they suggested for the physical monitoring aspect of the Project. For example, a persistent rumour had been circulating for many years about people receiving electrostatic-like shocks from megaliths. So, for instance, writing in 1974, Paul Screeton, journalist and former editor of *The Ley Hunter* magazine, and well known to us, recalled that from a stone at Hart, Cleveland, northern England, he "and several others have felt a tingling sensation of varying intensity" (Screeton 1974). Again, Jack Roberts, who was a co-worker with Martin Brennan in the study of the action of sunlight and shadow on Neolithic chambered mounds in Ireland (Brennan 1983), told me of a similar incident he experienced at Newgrange: he was entering the passage into the great Neolithic mound one morning and casually raised his hand to touch the lintel stone at the entrance as he passed underneath. He received a distinct shock that affected his whole arm. He gingerly reached out to touch the stone again, but this time nothing happened, as if the stone had 'discharged' itself.

A retired military officer, and a member of the National Trust, informed me of an occasion when he received a shock off one of the Rollright circle stones which, he said, left his forearm numb for about twenty minutes. In 1979, one of Pauline Flick's young volunteer site-wardens she maintained at the King's Men circle also told me, quite unprompted, that a stone in the circle had given him an "electric shock". We heard such reports from too many people to dismiss the effect. It really did seem that some stones can on occasion store up an electrostatic charge in some way, and that anecdotes like this could possibly be amenable to scientific enquiry.

In the course of its enquiries, principally at the Rollright Stones, the DPT noticed a few fleeting anomalies in passing that

Figure 5. The lintel stone above the passage entrance at the great Neolithic passage grave of Newgrange, Ireland. Above the lintel is the so-called 'roof box', through which the rising midwinter sun shines its rays down the entrance passage and into the central chamber – more on that later.

it never had time or resources to properly follow up. They are possibly of no consequence, but, on the other hand, they could potentially indicate much wider issues awaiting further research.

For instance, one recurring apparent anomaly involved electronic malfunctions especially involving quartz elements. During the Rollright energy research phase there, DPT personnel regularly reported how time-pieces and cameras containing quartz mechanisms would malfunction far more frequently within the King's Men circle than elsewhere. It became a widely noted and even joked-about phenomenon among volunteers. But it was something that tended to happen only during prolonged periods of time on site; such was the case during the 1990s when the Phoebus Cart company produced a Shakespeare play in the King's Men circle (about which more later): "Many cameras would jam or run out of battery power or films were blank when developed" (Mark Rylance, *personal communication*). And there was also the case of radio failures within the site. "We had one large 'shoe box' mobile phone and it did not work at all in proximity to the circle," says Rylance. These types of effect also frequently and noticeably occurred during DPT work at the site.

At one point, we received a special quartz lens on temporary loan from Kodak allowing for some ultra-violet photography, but apart from obtaining some dramatic images, we observed no unusual effects. But we also experimented for a while with infra-red film. Though little unusual or unexplained was found, we did obtain one odd photographic effect: a strange and subtle 'glow' around the tip of the King Stone (a specially heightened contrast image of this is shown on the opening page of Section One). This was at dawn, so could it have been the infra-red film detecting a warming of the stone? The Kodak physicist who joined us privately on a few occasions pointed out that the film was not sensitive far enough into the infra-red for this to be possible. But with the King Stone being silhouetted against the sky, could it be a tonal displacement artefact? The negative was closely analysed professionally and this was found not to be the case. (It should be mentioned here that a correspondent, Bernard Gowing, showed us an infra-red photograph he had taken of Kit's Coty House – an early Neolithic chambered barrow in Kent – showing a curious highly localised fog or haze hovering directly over the megalith, a phenomenon that had been invisible to the naked eye, Gower affirmed.)

Another anecdotal example was more of a surprise – it concerned ultrasound. It was initially prompted by contact I had with a zoologist prior to the formation of the Dragon Project; he told me of a colleague of his who had been studying bat behaviour one night on a country estate. At dawn, the man was returning to his base with a 'bat detector' (a wide-band ultrasonic receiver capable of detecting high-frequency sound such as that emitted by bats) still switched on. As he passed an ancient site on the estate, he noticed the receiver was registering a signal for which he could find no obvious cause. The zoologist passed the anecdote on to me for what it was worth. I recognized it as the usually suspect 'friend of a friend' type of anecdote, but, interestingly, this was later augmented after a fashion by John Barnatt, who, while engaged on surveying the henge of Arbor Low in Derbyshire, was interrupted by a man who wandered onto the site. He asked Barnatt if he knew why the skylarks frequented Arbor Low. On admitting that he had absolutely no idea, Barnatt was informed by the gentleman that it was due to "the ultrasound being emitted by the site's stones" (Barnatt, *personal communication*). Although slender coincidences, these anecdotes were felt by the Dragon Project coordinators to be sufficient to warrant obtaining wide-band ultrasonic receivers

Figure 6. A composite figure showing various examples of physical energy monitoring work taking place during the early years of the Dragon Project. (a) Monitoring for any infrared anomalies at the King's Men stone circle, Rollright. (b) Monitoring for infrared anomalies at the King Stone, Rollright. (Photo: Graham Challifour) (c) Roy Cooper using a Geiger counter at Rollright. (It took us much background monitoring to identify true radiation anomalies.) (d) Rodney Hale testing electrostatics at the tallest stone in the King's Men circle (the stone which produced ultrasonic anomalies). (e) Using a scintillometer to detect radioactivity at the King Stone. (f) Using a bat-detector type of ultrasound meter at Rollright.

of the 'bat-detector' type, and they were deployed on site on numerous occasions. A few ultrasonic anomalies were noted, a striking one being emissions of ultrasound from an approximately metre-wide band near the middle of the tallest, northernmost stone in the circle. For a while, this was a randomly repeated phenomenon occurring for about an hour always around dawn. No obvious explanation could be found, but it was speculated that possibly the stone was somehow heterodyning signals caused by microwave or other energy beams transmitted by distant communications towers brushing the ridge on which the King's Men is placed and catching the stone – the circle is, indeed, exposed to wide vista to the south. But who knows?

Introduction

TALES OF POWER

The further reason the DPT thought it to be worthwhile to look at potential energy properties of ancient sites was because such rumours are not confined to modern times and New Age notions.

The former inhabitants of our planet roamed their landscapes in cyclic, nomadic patterns. They knew where, when, and how to hunt; where to camp; where best to be at any given season; how to handle and work the natural materials in their environment and know what properties they possessed. They knew what plants to ingest for healing or for seeing visions. There was a general understanding, prior to the brief centuries of our present culture, that the Earth was alive, with subtle but powerful forces flowing through its body, the land. It was believed that these magical forces concentrated at various points which came to be regarded as totemic spots, sacred areas, or 'power places' as defined by the local culture. From astronomy to healing and the encounter with a perceived spirit world, the knowledge and wisdom of untold generations, distilled from empirical experience, was passed on through a variety of oral and ritual mnemonics. The shamans or Elders of every tribe knew where to go to have spiritual experiences – which holy ground, cave, spring, peak, or outcrop of rock.

For reasons that are not at all clear, the nomadic, flowing relationship with the land came to an end in Eurasia between about 9,000 and 5,000 years ago. Settlements developed; hunting and gathering gave way over a period of time to agriculture and farming. As if not to forget them, the old, natural sacred spots were sometimes marked or augmented with earth or stone. New sacred architecture arose. The intimate knowledge and abilities these ancient people had of the nature and usage of their materials still conjures awe in the modern visitor to the ruins of England's Stonehenge, Scotland's Callanish Stones, Ireland's Newgrange, America's Serpent Mound, Peru's Machu Picchu, Egypt's Great Pyramid, or the countless other remarkable works of ancient sacred engineering, large and small, the world over.

SITES OF THE DREAMTIME

Sufficient traditional vestiges remain today to illustrate these ancient tales of power, real or culturally imagined. We can take as an example of the early, natural relationship with the land the various tribes of Indigenous Australians, who, until recent times – and still fragmentarily today – led cyclic nomadic existences in their own lands, including following tribally significant mythic routes (so-called "song lines"). At points along these routes there were totemic sites. These 'Big Places' could be a particular hill, waterhole, large rock, quartz pavement, cave, rocky recess, or a special tree or bush. They were the places where the magical beings of the Dreamtime emerged from the ground, camped, performed a task, or where their forms are preserved in the shape of boulders and rock faces (simulacra – via pareidolia, a psychological phenomenon in which the mind responds to a stimulus, usually an image or a sound, by perceiving a familiar pattern where none exists). Each totemic place had its own song, ceremony and set of sacred objects (called *tapundas*, if wooden, and *tjinas* if made of stone). To Indigenous Australians, these sites were *increase centres*, from which the appropriate ritual could elicit the life essence or *kurunba* of living things, so ensuring the fecundity, the increase, of the particular plant or animal associated with the site. A.P. Elkin noted that "Unless the myths ... are preserved, the rites performed and the sites maintained as spirit sanctuaries, the living bond is broken, man and nature are separated, and neither man nor nature has any assurance of life in the future" (in Levy-Bruhl 1935).

Anthropologist and explorer, the late Charles P. Mountford, observed that the belief in a universal life essence was held by the Walbiri, Ngalia, Aranda, and Pitjantjara Aboriginal tribes, and that "the belief is probably far more widespread than existing literature indicates" (Mountford 1968). An important site on a totemic route of the Walbiri and Ngalia people is Ngama, a large rock outcrop near Mount Eclipse in central Australia. Various points and projections on the outcrop, and recesses and caves in it, have mythic significance to Indigenous Australians. A low, isolated rocky hill a few hundred metres west of this outcrop at Ngama was once the camp of Malatji, leader of the mythical dog-people. Every midwinter, tribesmen carry out an increase ritual at a boulder on the west side of this hill in which an Elder breaks off fragments of its flaking surface. "This action releases some of the *kurunba* contained in the rock," Mountford comments, "which flings in the air 'like a mist' and fertilizes the female dogs".

Of course, the sacred life of Indigenous Australians has been disrupted, and observances at the Big Places are now only kept up in a relatively fragmentary fashion. Very often the ritual objects secreted at Big Places have been found and stolen by Whites, and sold off.

AMERICAN INDIAN SACRED POWER

The Pueblo Indians of south-western USA have very similar understandings to Indigenous Australians, though their social structure took on a more organised nature. Like the Dreamtime entities, the Pueblo people believe they emerged from within the earth, and they feel themselves to be a part of nature and that the goal of human existence is to maintain that wholeness. Everything is sacred, so Pueblo shrines tend to blend with the landscape rather than being a place apart, in much the same manner as the Aboriginal totemic locations. Rina Swentzell, herself a Pueblo Indian, described one such shrine:

Last summer as I stood on Tsikumu, one of Santa Clara Pueblo's sacred mountains, I was most impressed by the wind, the beauty of the clouds and the flow of the hills below. There is a shrine on Tsikumu with a few well-placed stones which define an area scattered with cornmeal and a deeply-worn path in the bedrock. No special structure celebrates the sacredness of this place. Architecturally, it is understated, almost inconspicuous.

Tsikumu is typical of Pueblo shrines in that it is visually disappointing. It is, nevertheless, a special place because it is believed to be a place of access to the underworld from which the Pueblo people emerged. It is the doorway of communication between the many simultaneous levels of Pueblo existence. Tsikumu allows for a flow of energy between this plane of reality and other, concurrent, realities.

The shrines, boundary markers and centres, serve as constant reminders of the religious, symbolic nature of life. Because this physical realm of existence and other realms exist simultaneously, there is a constant flow between them. (Swentzell 1985.)

Like Indigenous Australians, the Pueblo Indians also recognize a life essence. They call it *Po-wa-ha*, which translates as 'water-wind-breath'. Swentzell states: "It is the breath which flows without distinction through the entirety of animate and inanimate existences" (*ibid.*). *Po-wa-ha* thus flows through places as well as people, animals, and plants.

Native American peoples of the Great Basin region (a vast area covering most of Nevada, much of Utah, as well as parts of California, Colorado, Idaho, Oregon and Wyoming) had shamanistic traditions that involved *puha* (presumably a version of *po-wa-ha*), an energy concept more or less identical to those of their Pueblo neighbours further south. Some rock art researchers (Huffman and Earley 2017, 2019) have identified ancient rock markings they think mark places of concentrated *puha*, depicting the Indians' visual idea of *puha* as serpentine lines (Figure 7).

Other Indian tribes to the north and east had similar ideas. The universal life essence to the Iroquois was *orenda*; to the Sioux it was *waken* or *wakonda*; and to the Crows it was *maxpe*.

THE MAGICAL POWER SYSTEMS OF OLD CHINA

The meaning of *Po-wa-ha/puha* is strikingly similar to that for the ancient Chinese system of geomancy or sacred geography – *Feng-shui*, which means 'wind-water'. Though the Chinese concept of natural forces or energies was sophisticated and complex, the basic similarity of the ideas is recognizable in the comments of a Victorian missionary to China, Ernest J. Eitel:

Figure 7. Ancient rock markings thought to express shamanic power
(*puha*) – lines and circles presumably representing *puha* currents and
nodes respectively. This example is at Snake Blakeslee in lower Apishapa
Canyon, Colorado. The researchers discovered it was a 'station' along an
Indian pilgrimage trail. [Photo courtesy of T.N. Huffman, F.L Earley.]

They (Feng-shui geomancers) see a golden chain of spiritual
life running through every form of existence and binding
together, as one living body, everything that subsists in
heaven above or on earth below. What has so often been
admired in the natural philosophy of the Greeks – that they
made nature live; that they saw in every stone, in every tree,
a living spirit; that they peopled the sea with naiads, the
forest with satyrs – this poetical, emotional and reverential
way of looking at natural objects, is equally so a characteristic of natural science in China. (Eitel 1873/1973).

Feng-shui, as it has come down to us, was practiced from at least early medieval times, and there is evidence indeed that its principles were being used up to 3,000 years ago in China. No dwelling or tomb would be built without a Feng-shui geomancer (*hsien-sheng*) studying the site and making necessary adjustment to the flow of energies there.

As Eitel explained:

> There are in the earth's crust two different, shall I say magnetic, currents, the one male, the other female; the one positive, the other negative ... The one is allegorically called the azure dragon, the other the white tiger ... This therefore is the first business of the geomancer on looking out for a propitious site, to find a true dragon, and its complement the white tiger, both being discernible by certain elevations of the ground ... in the angle formed by dragon and tiger, in the very point where the two (magnetic) currents which they individually represent cross each other, there may the luck-bringing site, the place for a tomb or dwelling, be found ... there must be there also a tranquil harmony of all the heavenly and terrestrial elements which influence that particular spot, and which is to be determined by observing the compass and its indication of the numerical proportions, and by examining the direction of the water courses. (Eitel, ibid.)

The Feng-shui compass, or *luopan* (Figure 8), is a complex affair, consisting of a central, magnetic compass needle surrounded by numerous circuits of symbols representing a range of conditions and aspects that had to be balanced together in the optimum case of site divination. The dragon and tiger symbols represented, respectively, the *yang* and *yin* forces within the earth, discernible by topography. These masculine and feminine principles occur throughout all creation in ancient Chinese cosmology, as in many others – the first principles emerging from the godhead, Tao, or whatever else one chooses to call the undifferentiated Divine Ground of existence.

Two basic schools of Feng-shui developed over the centuries: one concerned itself primarily with the actual lie of the land, while the other dealt with more abstract correspondences between philosophical and astrological principles. But in all cases, the key matter was the state of *ch'i* at a site. *Ch'i*, like *po-wa-ha, puha,* and *kurunba,* was considered to be a kind of universal essence or force, a 'cosmic breath' or 'life breath' that sustains all things. It was understood to operate at different scales. Acupuncture was the system developed to study and influence *ch'i* for human health; at the landscape level the system was Feng-shui. There are various *ch'i* in the heavens and earth, and an optimum balance of these was attempted at a site.

Figure 8. A Feng-shui compass (*luopan*).

In mountainous terrain, *ch'i* would rush vigorously; in flat, monotonous country it would become sluggish, stagnant. Feng-shui not only catalogued these characteristics, it also attempted to influence or control *ch'i*. So actual topographical modifications might be made at a location, with landscape engineering altering the slope of a hillside, for example. Similarly, water courses might be modified, trees planted, hollows scooped out of the ground, fountains or ponds installed. (Water was believed to carry *ch'i* and could be used to attract or contain it in an area; rushing, radiating, straight streams at a location, by the same token, would tend to disperse any *ch'i*.) Straight features – roads, water courses, ridges, rows and avenues of trees, railway lines, embankments, lines of posts, and so on – were 'secret arrows', causing *ch'i* to rush along them. A straight-line feature pointing at a dwelling, for example, would bring harmful influences into the home and had to be deflected, screened against or else mitigated by the judicious placing of a water feature. A straight linear feature running at right angles across the frontage of a house was also bad, because it was understood to drain away the site's *ch'i*. The obtaining of the right amount of *ch'i* at a site, in a balanced, harmonious condition, was the aim of the exercise. Too much, too little, too vigorous, too sluggish – all these *ch'i* states had to be avoided. As author Stephen Skinner has pointed out: "The essence of good feng-shui is to trap the ch'i energy flowing through the site and accumulate it without allowing it to go stagnant." (Skinner 1982)

Interestingly, while the populace avoided straight-line features under guidance of Feng-shui principles, the emperor in the Forbidden City at Beijing conducted his formal business on a throne situated at the focus of straight linear features, the most notable being the marbled meridian, the cosmic axis of the city. This apparent paradox actually yields some important clues regarding the mystery of ancient straight-line geomancy – see Pennick and Devereux 1989, or Devereux 2010. Straight lines and other inauspicious aspects of a site, such as corridors of cold, blustery winds or poor soil, for example, create conditions producing a negative form of *ch'i* called *sha*, as Skinner further explains: "Sha is the antithesis of ch'i and can be translated as 'noxious vapour'. (Skinner, ibid.)

Feng-shui has officially been discontinued in mainland China, but it still operates in such places as Hong Kong, Singapore, and Taiwan. The Feng-shui we now see is a hotch-potch of authentic traditional matter, common sense based on a close observation of the natural world, and rules and superstitions that have arisen for various reasons that have nothing to do with genuine principles of geomancy. An example of the latter is the Feng-shui dictum stating a narrow frontage on a house brings good luck, a notion that is a survival of a time when taxes on houses were assessed on their width!

The world is subject to quite different conditions and problems today, compared with those in old China (the electromagnetic environment, modern building materials, large-scale ecological effects of human activity, and so on), and it is wholly inappropriate for classical ideas of Feng-shui, complete with its now outmoded superstitions and local Chinese nuances and obsessions, to be simply plastered onto 21st-century circumstances elsewhere in the world. Nevertheless, if we cut through the superstitious or now irrelevant parts of Feng-shui, and attempt to see beyond what is to us rather colourful allegorical imagery and terminology, we can see that the core of the system is based on an intimate understanding of nature, including fairly sophisticated insights into geological, meteorological, medical, and architectural matters.

SOME OTHER NAMES OF POWER

People elsewhere in the world also believed in an invisible power. To the Pacific Islanders it was *mana,* a force that occupied both living and inanimate things. Its similarity to concepts of *kurunba, ch'i* or *po-wa-ha* is evident in this description of *mana*:

> It was the basic force of nature through which everything was done ...The comparison of mana with electricity, or physical energy, is here inescapable. The Polynesian conception of it was not scientific, of course, but it was otherwise completely logical. Mana was believed to be indestructible, although it might be dissipated by improper practices ... it flowed continuously from one thing to another and, since the cosmos was built on a dualistic idea, it flowed from heavenly things to earthbound things, just as though from a positive to a negative pole...
>
> Mana could be contained in any person or thing ... Chiefs were the main vessels, acting as contacts between god and man ... And, since mana flowed from high to low, an unguarded contact between a chief and a commoner was therefore an evil thing; the chief suffered a loss of mana ... and the commoner, with his limited capacity for mana, might be blown out like a fuse... (Howells 1948)

The deep, complex nature of the term has been more thoroughly and recently explored by Fox, Noyes, George and Laughlin (2018).

In North Africa, the force is known as *baraka*; to the ancient Greeks it was *pneuma*, to the Hindus, *prana*. Everywhere we look, earlier peoples had the concept of a force, or certain classes of energies, that moved through all things, and could also become focused at certain sacred places.

But what of European prehistory, the Stone Age, about which there is no direct documentation of such beliefs, or anything else? We can only act like detectives, sifting through bits and pieces of such evidence as we can find.

STONE AGE CLUES

We simply don't know if people held similar beliefs concerning an all-pervading force in Stone Age times, but we have various types of clue that suggest they may have done. The closest we can come to some Stone Age concept of an earth force being 'writ in stone' are perhaps the occasional examples of megaliths with serpentine lines carved at their bases, as if writhing up out of the earth. Two good examples of this are Stone 8, one of the uprights in the passage leading to the central chamber of the French passage grave of Gavrinis, and the base of an interior standing

Figure 9. The entrance façade of Gavrinis, Brittany.

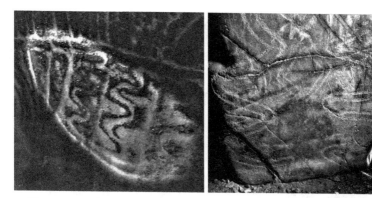

Figure 10. *Left*: The serpentine lines on the base of Stone 8 in Gavrinis.
Right: an interior stone (C16) in Barclodiad y Gawres, on Anglesey, Wales.
Could these lines depict a belief in an earth force, the *Nwyvre*, emanating
out of the ground and up into the stones?

stone (C16) inside the Neolithic chambered mound of Barclodi-ad-y-Gawres on the isle of Anglesey, Wales (Figure 10).

The late prehistorian, Aubrey Burl, speculated that the lines could in some way symbolise the earth (Burl 1985). This idea can be expanded with reference to what dregs of information we have regarding a belief about a serpent power, the *Wouivre* (*Vouivre*) or *Nwyvre*, held by the Iron Age Druids (Mereaux 1981). We do not know if the notion of *Nwyvre* originated in the Iron Age, or whether the Druids, who saw the closing chapters of prehistory in Europe, were in receipt of a much older (Neolithic or Mesolith-ic) belief, but it certainly would fit the Gavrinis and Barclodiad y Gawres markings.

And there are other examples of serpentine markings at other megalithic monuments. In Portugal, for example, there is the gargantuan collapsed passage grave called Anta Grande Do Zambujeiro (Figure 11) where one of the huge, formerly upright stones has its surface covered in a seething mass of barely visible wriggling lines.

Figure 11. The mighty, collapsed megalithic structure of Anta Grande Do Zambujeiro, Portugal, said to be Europe's largest dolmen (now under protective covering). One of the now leaning large (c.4m/14ft) stones, has its surface covered in fine wriggling lines – not amenable to photography, unfortunately.

There are doubtless other examples, at least along the western fringes of Europe, but no one has as yet produced a detailed and comprehensive survey of such markings.

For a further chance to peer back through the mists of deep time, we have no option but to look at what exists of oral, and subsequently written, folklore in the hope that actual recall of the Stone Age ideas of an earth force may be partially contained within it, however fragmented and distorted.

ECHOES FROM ANTIQUITY?

Looking specifically at folklore related to prehistoric and ancient sites, we can discern perhaps ten basic legendary themes that could possibly be echoes of beliefs in antiquity, or at least of an inchoate folk recognition of there being certain sites with curious properties. We'll look at British sites as their lore is particularly well chronicled.

Healing

Healing lore is mainly associated with stones and water. A classic megalithic example is Men-an-Tol in Cornwall. Children suffering from rickets (a disorder causing fragile or soft bones) would be passed three or nine times through the stone's hole. In some versions, the patient was dragged three times around the stone against the sun (widdershins).

Several other holed stones around the country had similar traditions. The stones of Stonehenge also supposedly had healing properties, obtained by splashing water on them and making a bath or infusion from the liquid. The written form of this rumour goes back to at least the 12th Century when

Figure 12. Men-an-Tol, Cornwall. (Now found to have been part of a stone circle.)

Geoffrey of Monmouth recorded the "healing virtue" of the monument's stones.

Many ancient holy wells were also thought to have healing properties – the taking of the waters could be good for a wide range of ailments, though 'sore eyes' seems to have been the major condition treated! While these may not be thought to be prehistoric sites, most authorities agree that many of these wells and springs were venerated in at least late prehistoric times, the process simply becoming Christianised later. Indeed, the veneration of water is likely to have come down from remotest antiquity.

Movement

Supernatural movement is specifically associated with stones. Variations on the theme are that a particular standing stone or set of stones would go down to a nearby stream to drink, or run around the field, or rise up out of the ground and rotate "when they hear a clock strike midnight", "when the cock crows", "at noon", or

Figure 13. The Hoarstone, Enstone, Oxfordshire. [Photo: Mark Turner]

at particular times of the year. Similar lore is attached to a stone of the King's Men circle at Rollright. Leslie Grinsell (1976) wryly pointed out that the Hoarstone, near Enstone, Oxfordshire, not far from the Rollright Stones, is supposed to go to drink when it hears the church clock at Lidstone strike midnight, yet Lidstone church does not have a striking clock!

A counter-theme of this motif is that certain stones cannot be moved by human agency or, if they are so displaced, will either return automatically or else cause such problems that the person involved will feel obliged to return the stone, and find it curiously easy to do so.

Petrifaction

According to this undoubtedly Christianised theme, the stones at some sites are people who have been turned to stone, usually for working, playing, or otherwise transgressing the Sabbath. An example is the stone circle complex at Stanton Drew, Avon, where the stones were deemed to be members of a wedding party whose dancing went on through the night and into Sunday. The hired fiddler declined to continue after midnight, but a stranger appeared who offered to play on until dawn. This was, naturally, the Devil. The people were duly turned to stone, and will only be released from their petrological bondage when the Devil comes to play for them again. Another classic example of this folkloric theme is associated with the Merry Maidens stone circle in Cornwall (Figure 14).

Countless Stones

Grinsell (ibid.) noted that this theme was attached to at least eleven stone circles or other megalithic structures in Britain. The basic legend states that the stones at these places cannot be

Figure 14. The Merry Maidens stone circle, Cornwall.

properly counted. Each time one tries, a different number will be arrived at. Folklore records that certain individuals, in an attempt to circumvent this frustrating situation, would take a given number of loaves to a site, and place one on each stone, with the aim of counting the loaves left. However, the Devil always spoiled such attempts by surreptitiously creeping up behind the person knocking the placed loaves to the ground. An instance of this folklore is attached to the King's Men stone circle at Rollright.

Desecration

As if a protective curse has been laid on them, it is stated in lore that many prehistoric sites will bring bad luck or even death upon anyone disturbing them. There are many traditions to this effect, and numerous anecdotal accounts that claim people actually have experienced misfortune after destroying a site.

A sub-theme of this motif links monuments with meteorology: people disturbing these sites can expect to be subjected to severe weather conditions such as freak winds or fierce electrical storms. Folklore aside, there are a number of accounts of this actually happening. In 1849, for instance, when Dean Merewether of Hereford and his team were digging at Silbury Hill near Avebury in Wiltshire, a "dramatic high Gothick thunderstorm" broke out, and men working deep within the great mound felt it shudder to its base. The Dean wryly observed that the significantly timed storm was "much to the satisfaction ... of the rustics". It can't help but be remarked on that when a major, and probably final excavation commissioned by Heritage England into the heart of Silbury Hill was conducted by archaeologists and contractors in 2007, work was severely hampered and ultimately delayed by exceptional stormy weather.

Another anecdote was supplied by a farmer who told Lewis Edwards in the 1940s that when he approached Carreg-y-Bucci (the Hobgoblin Stone) on top of a prehistoric mound near Lampeter, Wales, with the intention of breaking it up for gateposts, "there was a violent thunderstorm, the worst I have ever known. I ran for my life, but it followed me all the way home".

Figure 15. The Neolithic artificial mound of Silbury Hill, Wiltshire. Silbury is to the left in this view, the natural ridge of Waden Hill is at right.

Figure 16. Major excavations at Silbury Hill in 2007 were temporarily
stalled by exceptionally wet conditions.

Three men have reportedly been killed by lightning alongside the
stone (Edwards 1949).

Fairies

Fairies and other elemental entities were traditionally thought
to inhabit particular prehistoric sites. These places were usually prehistoric earthen mounds, but megaliths were sometimes
involved. A classic fairy site is Willy Howe, Humberside – a large
Neolithic mound that from at least medieval times was considered a fairy mound, and travellers passing that way at night would
be on their guard if they heard the sounds of revelry coming from
the barrow. In the 12th Century, William of Newburgh recorded
that a local countryman saw an opening in the mound one night
and on peering in saw a fairy banquet in progress. He was offered
a cup of wine, but the man knew his lore better than to drink or
eat fairy food or enter the magically illuminated fairy domain

lest he become enchanted. We might say in today's terminology that that would mean he would experience a time warp, the 'Rip Van Winkle effect', often reported by UFO abductees (a kind of modern fairylore). He threw away the drink but ran off with the cup, much to the outrage of the fairies. The cup was said to be of unknown material, of an unusual colour and shape, and to have passed into the possession of Henry the Elder.

Ireland is of course well known for its fairy forts and 'raths' (usually Iron Age or medieval fortified dwelling sites). A fine example is Lios Ard in County Mayo. Folklore concerning fairies have long been associated with this place, and even in recent memory people have reported seeing sightings of strange figures, some with "penetrating staring eyes", busying themselves on and around the mound (Mac Manus 1959/1973).

As we will see later in this book, *lights* were also reportedly seen at some ancient sites, and these were typically referred to as fairies by countryfolk.

Figure 17. Lios Ard fairy mound, Kiltimagh, Co. Mayo.

Treasure

Prehistoric mounds and stone circles were frequently reported to contain treasure. Willy Howe also had this legend attached to it: the story goes that people dug into the mound to reach a chest of gold. They attached a chain and horses to it, but the harder the animals pulled, the deeper the chest sank into the barrow. An almost identical tale is attached to another prehistoric barrow, Mutlow Hill in Essex, the treasure there being a golden coach. A great many other sites around the country are said to conceal treasure. In some cases, dragons guarded hordes of riches.

Strange lights figure again in treasure lore. The Iron Age earthworks on Trencrom Hill, Cornwall, are supposed to harbour giants' treasure. It is said that a tin miner two hundred or so years ago saw lights on the hill and climbed up to find a long passage, along which was unguarded gold. (Interestingly, it was traditional up to the early years of the 20th Century amongst some miners of copper, tin, and other metals to look for light phenomena emerging from the ground, as that was said to indicate the presence of good veins of ore. See Devereux 1989).

In many countries, in Europe and South America particularly, curious lights that appear repeatedly in the same area are said to mark the position of buried treasure. Denmark had a strong tradition of these treasure lights, at least until the 18th Century, and in Germany if treasure is buried at a ruined site, blue flames or globes of light mark the location. In Peru, treasure lights are called *la loz del dinero* ('the money lights'), and in Brazil, *Mae de Ouro* ('Mother of Gold').

Perhaps the real treasure was a different kind of wealth.

Ghosts

It is almost to be expected that some folklore would claim that there were spectres at ancient places. These stories usually involve castles and old houses, but some have been associated with prehistoric sites. A particularly interesting legend involves the apparition of a gigantic golden figure seen at the barrow of Bryn-yr-Ellyllon ('the Hill of Goblins') near Mold in North Wales. This old story seems to have pre-dated the discovery of a gold corselet found when the mound was cleared in 1833. If this is in fact the case, then it would seem that relatively specific memories can indeed be encapsulated in lore down a great many generations.

A phantom horseman was seen on Bottlebush Down in Dorset in the winter of 1927-1928 by the archaeologist, Dr. R.C.C. Clay. The galloping figure was clad in flowing clothes and shook a spear at Clay who, shocked, was observing from a moving car. The horseman suddenly vanished and Clay stopped and went over to the spot, to find a Bronze Age round barrow that he hadn't previously noticed. On another occasion, again on Bottlebush, a person who rested on a barrow claimed to have found himself surrounded by "little people in leather jerkins", and yet again on the Down, a shepherd also saw a phantom horseman appear from behind a clump of shrubs near a prehistoric earthwork (Harte 1986; Pennick and Devereux 1989). (Bottlebush Down is crossed by one of the largest and most enigmatic types of earthworks of the Neolithic period – a six-mile-long *cursus*, formed by parallel lines of ditches and banks, nowadays best seen from the air.)

Mysterious lights also figure in this folklore motif. Six independent witnesses told antiquarian G. Wilson in the 1880s that they saw, on repeated occasions, a light move from Torhouskie Cairn in Scotland to a stone on top of a water conduit. The stone supposedly had been taken from the cairn, so the light was believed to be claiming its own. The old Scandinavians would not have been surprised: "lambent flames" issuing from burial cairns were a part of their folklore too – their name for the lights was *haug-eldir*.

Fertility

Prehistoric symbolisation of fertility occurred in the case of standing stones by the fact that they can look phallic. This is explicitly depicted at some sites. In the graveyard of Aghowle church in County Wicklow, Ireland, for instance, is a 1.5-m (5-ft) stone in the form of a phallus (though its glans has now been destroyed). And the Lia Fáil, the Stone of Destiny, on the Hill of Tara in Ireland, was perhaps the ultimate fertility stone: at the coronation of the ancient pagan kings of Ireland the rightful monarch had to touch the stone, and if it let out a sound, it confirmed the kingship. In the archaic concept of sovereignty, it was believed that the king and the land were one, with the fertility of the king being indivisibly bound up with that of the land. The Lia Fáil stands proud on the Hill of Tara, but what many visitors miss is the view of the prehistoric stone pillar from above – there is a hole representing the urethra in its top (Figure 18), confirming its already suggestive phallic nature.

Such prehistoric phallic stones occur in several countries. One such exists at Tømmerby in Denmark, and several stone phalli rising to 3m (10ft) occur near Soddu in southern Ethiopia. And in ancient Mexico there was a cult producing very explicit phallic stones (Figure 19). Little is known about the cult, but it was seemingly introduced into Mayan culture from the Veracruz area of the Gulf of Mexico towards the close of the Classic

Figure 18. (a) The Lia Fáil on the Hill of Tara. (b) The view from above, showing the hole representing the urethra, thus confirming the phallic nature of the monolith.

Period, c.959-1539 A.D., and thence spread to various parts of the Maya domain.

Stone symbols of fertility were not confined to phallic ones, of course – vulvic symbols also were created. One of the more explicit stone-age examples can be found on a stone in an inner setting within the Avebury henge (Figure 20). It is often bypassed unnoticed by visitors nowadays, but in Neolithic times it may possibly have been considered as identifying the stone as a fertility goddess. Because we have no documentation from Neolithic times, we can only infer.

Even purely natural formations may have been invested with meaning. For example, there is a spur or promontory jutting out southwards from the Carn Menyn ridge in the Preseli Hills of South Wales, the source area of the Stonehenge bluestones. This spur was cordoned off by a low linear feature formed by earth and small rocks in prehistoric times, creating a kind of temenos (Darvill 2006 and *personal communication*). Near the centre of this spur there is a naturally occurring massive granite block. On its top surface there

Figure 19. A tall, cultic phallus stone near the Mayan ritual cave of Balankanché in the Yucatán, Mexico. It originally stood a few miles away from this precise location.

is a naturally-formed vulvic-shaped depression (Figure 21). Was this taken as imbuing the rock with sanctity, with being a sign of the earth goddess's presence?

As we will see, entire mountains with certain configurations could be taken as symbolising, even as *being*, the earth goddess residing in the landscape.

* * * * *

There are, of course, many more examples of folkloric motifs, and there are numerous other aspects of folklore attached to prehistoric sites (Grinsell identifies almost thirty), but these latter have themes certainly or most probably originating in the historical era, such as Arthurian associations, etymological explanations, Christianised tradition, assemblies, and so forth.

Figure 20. A vulvic image occurs on this standing stone in the henge at Avebury. It is primarily formed from natural folds in the rock, but so explicit is it that one cannot help but suspect the form was enhanced by human hand.

Figure 21. The vulvic-shaped feature in the stone block on the Carn
Menyn promontory.

Folklore was the mnemonic system of country people; it was
designed for the rural hearth on dark winter evenings to help
explain the mysterious stones and earthworks with which these
people shared the landscape. While rulers came and went, the
peasant population remained, by and large, fairly intact, until the
great scattering caused by the Industrial Revolution. Even today,
folklore is still passed on in areas that have retained some degree
of rural integrity. Legends are like time capsules, and germs of
truth and ancient ideas can be conveyed within elaborate imagery
and spurious story-telling. It is just conceivable that the folklore
themes outlined above contain hints of genuine information if
they can be deciphered. The ideas that stones can *move* in a variety of ways, that they are petrified people, and that they can evade
being counted, suggest an underlying sense that the stones have
something *animate* about them, that they possess some strange

agency – a narrative possibly predicated on a now lost belief that the old stones are alive in some way.

The various motifs dealing with fairies, ghosts, lights, and enchantment suggest the possibility of underlying observations of generations of local people that unusual phenomena have been seen or associated with stone circles and similar places. Folklore is highly complex and can rarely be taken at face value: it is eclectic, gathering its images and rationale from many sources. The surface of folklore is regularly embellished, long after the possible meanings of the fundamental motifs have been forgotten. Yet it is these legendary cores that are the important components of folklore, and if one sums up those aspects of the themes itemised above, the general sense comes across that the old stones and other anciently venerated places have been regarded as being associated with archaic concepts of *power*, of unusual, even supernatural, phenomena, which took culturally varied forms around the ancient world. While we should not accept folklore literally, neither should we dismiss it too readily until we have mined whatever germs of ancient memory it might contain.

PART ONE

PHYSICAL ENERGIES
AND ANOMALIES

Section Introduction

There are numerous reasons that determined the placement of ancient sacred sites in the landscape, some of them cultural or mythological, topographical, or pragmatic (such as being locations of natural materials for ceremonies, or hunting lookouts, or memorials of actual or mythic events, and so forth). But with traditional folklore and modern anecdotes hinting that there were and are strange energetic effects at *some* ancient, usually prehistoric, sites and venerated natural places, the Dragon Project took it upon itself in the late 1970s to investigate these ideas further, as much as it was able, to see if there was any identifiable basis to such rumours. There was no assumption that all monumental or sacred sites possessed anomalistic energy effects.

The physical investigations were an effort that lasted, sporadically, for over a few years. At this stage there was no intent to seek some fugitive, mystical universal force, but rather to explore physical, measurable forces which, in the past, may have given rise to more fanciful notions. But what forces would they be?

Sites really need to be monitored continuously for measurable energy properties, compared with control locations, for months or years at a stretch, but the Project's resources simply did not, and do not, exist for such unorthodox work to be carried out at this level. All we could do was to look at a representative selection of what had so far been measured or observed. Even Rollright, which, as we have noted, was for some years field headquarters of the DPT, has by no means had a thorough study of whatever geophysical properties it might have. Energy findings at other monuments have resulted, variously, from chance observations to planned sessions of several hours of monitoring.

Knowledge of transient phenomena, or phenomena that has only just begun to be noticed, of necessity relies on chance human observation. Some types of energy effects are, therefore, recorded in this section anecdotally. There is no way of avoiding this if the record is to be maintained. But the cases I have included are based on what I am satisfied are reliable accounts. Others I am less confident about I have omitted and, of course, I have no doubt people have had numerous other experiences that have not come to my notice.

The Dragon Project initially decided upon magnetism and radiation (i.e. natural, background, radioactivity) for the physical monitoring, but eventually included light phenomena, and, more recently, sound (it is often forgotten that this, too, is a physical force).

The Rollright Stones were used to test a wide variety of monitoring approaches, mainly because it was the Project's field base in the early years, and so will have recurring mentions in the following pages. Most other sites had only preliminary and partial checks. It was all just a beginning, and that remains the case these many years later, but a start of accountable research had to be made: it was decided that pet theories or elaborate speculations based on the wanderings of dowsing rods really would no longer suffice.

Of the four main areas of energy effect referred to above, only the light phenomena are likely to relate to a currently unexplored energy – possibly an exotic form of plasma. The others are well known to science and might seem somewhat mundane to fans of such movies as *Raiders of the Lost Ark* or *Romancing the Stone*. There is nothing paranormal about these forces, but we are looking at them in a context not studied by mainstream science, and it is that context which is important and holds the promise of revealing what may have been a prehistoric knowledge and usage of the effects of natural energies. *This could have its own archaeology if we have the wit to identify it.*

A mere beginning was made on a formidable task by the DPT, and there has been precious little accountable such research since. The study of noteworthy, measurable energy effects at prehistoric sites is in a state similar to that of aeronautics prior to 1904: there have been a few string-and-sealing-wax trials but many more claims relying on hot air.

The sites referred to in the following pages are primarily (though not exclusively) British sites, for the simple reason they are the ones where most research results have so far been obtained. Basic background information is given on each of the main types of energy investigated, followed in each case by a few site examples.

Finally, to reiterate, no claim is being made that all prehistoric sites have an association with physical energies by any means, but rather that some do.

Natural (Background) Radioactivity

It is difficult nowadays to talk about radioactivity without images of Chernobyl, Three Mile Island, Sellafield or Fukushima being conjured before the mind's eye. But nuclear power stations (not to mention nuclear weaponry) are purely technological constructs involving radiation levels conjured into an intensity not normally encountered in nature – not terrestrial nature at any rate. It is not these high levels of radiation that concern us here.

Natural ionizing radiation (including alpha and beta particles, gamma rays, X-rays) pervades the whole environment. Beyond certain levels radiation is, as we know, harmful to human beings and other living things. The levels ('dose') that are considered safe or acceptable are subject to social, medical and political rules and laws.

Natural radioactivity in our immediate environment comes from both terrestrial and astronomical sources. Cosmic rays constantly bombard our atmosphere from deep space and from the sun. These interact with particles in the upper atmosphere causing secondary particles to rain down in shifting amounts. Radiation levels increase with altitude and also with latitude because more cosmic rays enter our atmosphere near the poles than the equator due to the shape of the envelope of the Earth's magnetic field. Beneath our feet, numerous components of the Earth's crust are radioactive, notably uranium, thorium, and potassium-40. These are dispersed through the ground in variable concentrations. Even vegetation can have radioactive properties because it grows out of the ground. Bananas, for instance, are radioactive due to potassium-40 (there is even an informal dosage level known as the 'banana dose' or BED!), as are numerous other foodstuffs – Brazil nuts in particular.

One of the decay products of uranium is the radioactive gas, *radon* (radon-222), which can emerge from the ground into the atmosphere. The igneous rock granite can be particularly radioactive, and areas where granite outcrops extensively, or where large amounts of the stone are used as a building material (Scotland's 'granite city' of Aberdeen, for example), will have higher radon counts than places with less granite. Radon can accumulate in granite-built houses without good ventilation and become a health hazard.

The Dragon Project and radiation monitoring

It is estimated by the National Radiological Protection Board (NRPB) in the UK that in the average annual radiation dose received by the population, gamma-rays account for 16 per cent of the total dose, cosmic rays for 13 per cent, and radon for 33 per cent. Radon dosage of course varies from area to area depending on geology. Indeed, the official comprehensive monitoring of radiation dosage out of doors only began in Britain as relatively recently as 1980 – two years after the commencement of fieldwork on the Dragon Project, as it happens. The NRPB took at least one measurement in every $10km^2$ of the Ordnance Survey grid. While this gives a good overall picture of regional variations in radiation throughout the British Isles, it does not address the much more detailed information the Dragon Project needed in order to try to work out how genuine radiation anomalies at sites might be identified. It obliged the Project to take hundreds of Geiger counter readings overall in order to be able to determine what an unusual high or low radiation count would be at any given site compared with its regional environment.

While occasionally the Project had access to more sophisticated radiation monitoring equipment by means of begging and borrowing, limited financial resources meant that it primarily used simple radiation monitors (basic types of Geiger counters), which issue audible clicks in reading radiation levels. These detectors record essentially random events, and averages of their readings have to be used to give meaningful information. Primitive perhaps, but workable. Therefore, readings were taken at sites and in their environments for precisely timed periods of minutes or hours, then averaged to *counts per minute* (CPM). While CPM can theoretically be converted to specific units of radiation measurement, the work proceeded with CPM, and consisted mainly of comparing selected ancient sites with local background measurements, and in some cases with readings taken elsewhere. While the use of CPM does not provide quantitative radiation dosage information, it is adequate for comparing radiation levels at sites, backgrounds and control locations, thus revealing if levels are unusual at a given site. It also allows for comparison percentages to be used.

The Gaia Programme

This was a particular programme set up within the overall effort of the DPT designed to take radiation readings at numerous

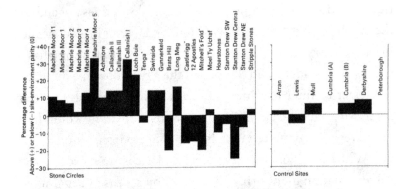

Figure 22. Histogram allowing comparison of averaged radiation counts
between the 25 stone circles monitored on the Dragon Project's 'Gaia
Programme', expressed in percentage terms above or below their respective averaged background readings. (The three stone circles asterisked
are known to possess stones that strongly affect magnetic compasses
– it is possibly noteworthy that they are all sites with radiation averages
below that of their environments.)

sites and their backgrounds around the UK to see if any pattern
emerged. The outcome is shown in the histogram (Figure 22).

When the results of the Gaia programme were processed in
1988, no sign of any consistent pattern showed up, but interesting results were nevertheless obtained – the findings do generally
show a difference between stone circle readings and those taken
at randomly selected control locations in the open landscape.

The procedure for taking readings at both actual sites and
control locations and their environments was always virtually identical. Every column on the histogram has resulted from
around 40-50 individual readings totaling hours of actual
monitoring time. The vertical scale on both histograms is the
same, allowing direct comparison. Volunteer monitors on the
programme were asked to do at least one 'dummy' (control) place
per region in which the actual prehistoric sites were monitored.

The main histogram shows the site-to-environment relationships in terms of percentage differences. If site and surroundings
gave the same averaged radiation readings, there is no column,
the difference being zero. A difference in readings between site
and local environment is unexpected, but in the event, as we can
see, stone circle sites differed in radiation terms up to 33 per cent
from their environments. While there is no meaningful statistical pattern overall in these results, there is at least a hint that
natural background radiation levels seem in some way modified
in the presence of megalithic groupings.

But as the Project was limited in its resources, it could not
maintain extended monitoring work, and until large numbers
of sites can be continuously monitored for very long periods,
we cannot be sure that whatever variations are perceived are
not due simply to random fluctuations in background radiation
levels. The nearest we have so far come to such a situation was in
a unique radiation monitoring experiment carried out by DPT
volunteers Cosimo and Ann Favaloro at Easter Aquorthies, a
19.5-m (64-ft) diameter recumbent stone circle in Aberdeen-
shire, north-east Scotland.

At Easter Aquorthies

A recumbent circle is one with a stone in its circumference lying
flat, often appearing like a massive altar flanked by uprights.
There are over ninety of these sites in north-east Scotland, and
there have been suggestions that some of them might be aligned
to the moon at the point known as the 'major lunar standstill'
in its 18.6-year cycle. In the year of a major lunar standstill, the
winter full-moonrise will reach its northernmost position, and in
the same year the summer full-moonrise will reach its southern-

most point. The height of the moon's journey across the sky in such a year also varies dramatically: to the observer the moon can arc high overhead one month and be seen skimming along the horizon during another. Prehistorian Aubrey Burl felt that some of the recumbent circles may have related to these extreme lunar positions for ceremonial effect – so, for example, a major standstill-period low moon might seem from a position within the circle to 'roll' across the (often perfectly horizontal) surface of the recumbent stone.

Burl suggested Easter Aquorthies as one of the recumbent sites having probable major lunar-standstill significance. 1987 was a major lunar-standstill year, and 29 September was one of the important dates of that year (a moonset), so that was when the Favaloros arranged to be at the site.

They conducted both instrumental and human-response experiments, but here we need consider only their radiation monitoring. They used two DPT instruments specially designed

Figure 23. The recumbent stone at Easter Aquorthies – note its altar-like appearance.

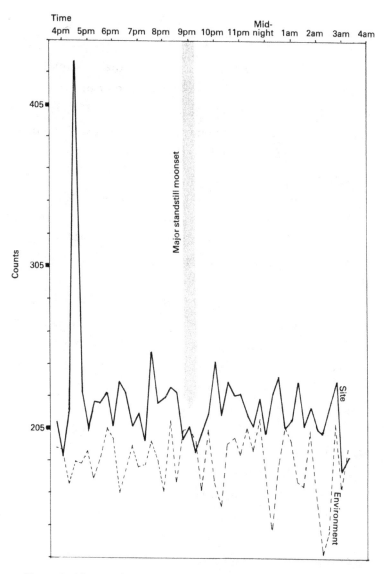

Figure 24.This graph depicts almost 12 hours of continuous radiation
monitoring at the Easter Aquorthies site (solid bold line) simultaneous
with its environment (broken line). The dramatic 'flare up' of readings
at the site around 4.45PM is clearly observable, as is the major period of
overlap of the two sets of readings occurring just at the time of moonset.
See text for further discussion [After Favaloro].

to monitor background radiation that kept automatic counts. One was positioned inside the circle, the other was placed at a point at a distance in the environment. The two instruments were run simultaneously, and readings taken from them simultaneously at 15-minute intervals over an almost 12-hour period, from 3.45 pm on 29 September to 2.45 am the next morning. The moon set at 9 pm, so the monitoring period bracketed the event by several hours. Not only did this experiment represent the longest continuous period of simultaneous site-andenvironment radiation monitoring so far undertaken, it was quite unique in that the period covered such a significant lunar event.

We can see the outcome in Figure 24. Two noteworthy things are indicated. The first is that at 4.30 pm on 29 September, there was an extraordinary flare-up of readings at the site while the environment remained normal. This increase was of considerable relative magnitude as can be seen and demonstrates clearly that background radiation levels can change at a site while the surroundings are not affected.

The rest of the graph shows that throughout almost the entire period, the site (solid line) registered higher readings than the surroundings (broken line), while a major overlap between the two sets of readings occurred *precisely over the moonset period*. For this to have happened only at this point during the course of twelve hours makes it difficult to dismiss as mere coincidence.

Finally, it can be seen that for most of the period there was a tendency, though not an exact pattern, for site readings to increase around the times the background readings were decreasing. These results overall should give everyone interested in ancient sites, from whatever viewpoint, food for thought.

BIOLOGICAL RESPONSE TO RADIOACTIVITY

Modern science states that "ionising radiation cannot be directly detected by the human senses" (NRFB 1988). This may be true for the five senses as such, but it seems that living organisms can have biological means of being aware of radiation. There are a few fragments of research and experience that relate to this as yet poorly understood area.

The author and researcher Lyall Watson described work of the early 1960s that shows that humble creatures like worms can sense radiation:

> Frank Brown has tested his planarian worms for response to a very weak gamma radiation emitted by a sample of cesium 137. He found that worms were aware of the radiation and turned away from it, but only when they were moving north or south. They ignored the radiation, no matter where it came from, if they were swimming in any other direction. This shows that gamma rays can be a vector force that somehow indicates direction as well as intensity. (Watson 1974)

If other living things can sense or react to radiation, perhaps human beings also possess biological means that subtly inform the body of ambient radiation levels. If so, the old shamans may have been able to develop and refine such an ability and directly sense energy from some stones. Radiation is of course inherently harmful to living tissue. Exposure to high levels of natural radioactivity can cause illness and death, but perhaps much lower – we might say 'homeopathic' – and short doses of radiation, could have *curative* effects. (As the 16th-century alchemist

Paracelsus put it: "The poison is the dose".) This controversial idea is known as 'radiation hormesis'. This is reputedly the case in Boulder, Montana, USA, where old gold and uranium mines have been used for giving sufferers of certain ailments strictly-timed periods of exposure to the radon concentrations in the abandoned workings. There are claims that the radon atmosphere has helped in cases of arthritis and the control of blood sugar in diabetics, amongst other illnesses. Orthodox medicine challenges such claims, naturally, but one woman user of the radon environment provided by the mines stated that she has been able to dispense with the wheelchair she had to use and can now happily walk unaided up and down the mine level while she is being exposed to her timed dose of radon (CNN 1987). Decades ago, in America, 'radon kits' were sold for healing purposes, with radon being contained in canisters from which the purchaser could take supposedly healthful sniffs! At the beginning of the 20th Century, radioactive caves in Colorado were used for health visits by some Americans in just the same way that their European counterparts would visit spas. But perhaps the two activities were not so dissimilar if one thinks of the radioactive status of the sacred waters at Bath, England, for instance (see below). If certain levels of, or exposure to, natural radiation can stimulate healing in certain types of disorder, healing lore connected with particular standing stones sites could perhaps be explained.

Dartmoor, in southern England, a granite upland with generally heightened background radiation levels, has its own reputation. The antiquarian, S. Baring-Gould, in his *A Book of Dartmoor* (1900), made a special mention of what he called the "salubrity" of the moor, noting that it had become "a thing not unusual" during his day for those suffering from a "delicacy of the lungs" to stay on a farm or cottage on the moor. He also cited a physician at Dartmoor Prison remarking in a report in the early 1800s that the exceptionally good health of the prisoners was an "anomaly", defying the appalling prison conditions and the "cheerless and hyperborean" moor. I have myself experienced such 'salubrity' on a couple of occasions when being on the moor for many hours. The first was years ago when studying a long prehistoric stone row on Ugborough Moor (on the southern reaches of Dartmoor). Tracking across difficult terrain with a substantial backpack, I suddenly somehow 'switched' from my usual puffing and panting efforts into a much faster rhythm of walking, covering great strides with absolute ease, breathing as calmly as if I was seated in a chair. I rapidly overtook my two fitter, more outdoor-type companions who I had been trailing behind, much to their amazement. This was far more than 'second wind', which I have often experienced in fieldwork; if anything, it seemed something similar to the trance walking called *lung-gom* in Tibet (David-Neel 1932).

On a considerably later occasion, my wife and I had been spending long and tiring days studying the stone row complexes on the Drizzlecombe and Shovel Down parts of the moor, yet on each day we both felt increasingly invigorated and charged with energy as we worked – in fact, against all logic, we left the moor decidedly more energetic than when we started out in the mornings.

'Spook Road'

I have come to the view that certain types of slightly heightened radiation environments can possibly help trigger a specific range of psycho-spiritual experiences in some people – hallucinations or visions, however one chooses to describe them. An old country ridgeway and county boundary (formally the course of a tradition-al gypsy route around the country) running alongside Rollright's King's Men stone circle became nicknamed by Dragon Project operatives as 'spook road' for reasons that will become clear.

A stretch of this road about 360m (1200ft) long has been found to average over three times the levels of the normal radiation background. Although it is just possible that this effect is caused by some radioactive mineral geologically deposited in a thin strip along the top of the ridge where the road happens to run, it is much more likely to be due to radioactive elements in the road's foundation material, such as granite chippings, beneath that part of the road. But no matter how caused, the higher radiation levels of that strip of road are natural and were initially found out only by chance because of the Project's detailed energy research going on at and around the Rollright Stones. It was also only because of the work going on at the stones that volunteers involved in site-en-

Figure 25. Airview of the King's Men stone circle, Rollright, and adjacent country road. The King Stone can be seen in the upper right-hand corner of the frame

ergy studies found themselves walking on that part of the road at various times of the day. Three of them, strangers to one another and on site at different times, independently handed me accounts of curious experiences they had on the road – at that time I alone knew that all three had their reported experiences precisely on the radioactive stretch of the road. The people involved were known to me over many years and I judge them to be totally reliable.

The first reported event took place on 16 February, 1980. The percipient was Roy Cooper, formerly an Oxford University surveyor. At the time the experience took place, there had been a large group of researchers at the Rollright Stones since the early hours of the morning. At 9 am, Roy left the stone circle and the buzz of activity there to walk out onto the road to his car, which was parked in the lay-by near the site's entrance gate:

> As I left the circle through the gate, I saw a car approaching … approximately half a mile away. I paid little heed to it. It appeared to be travelling 35-40mph, and I noticed it again as I reached my own car parked in the lay-by. I opened the boot [trunk] of my car (two seconds?) and suddenly realised the approaching car, with two occupants, had disappeared. The disappearance struck me much more forcibly than any impression of the importance of the car initially. It certainly had not stopped in the lay-by and no way had it had time to disappear around the next bend (300-400 yards away) … Either the car had disappeared or, somehow, I had suffered a time lapse. Usually I'm a very good judge of time, seldom wear a watch and can normally judge the time within five minutes at any time of the day and often at night as well. *The distinct and overriding impression I had was that the car had disappeared* [Cooper's emphasis]. I've never experienced anything of this nature before … The

experience was so odd that I decided to keep it to myself until the end of the monitoring period. (Personal communication, 1980.)

I was dumbfounded to receive a letter from someone else telling of another 'odd' event on the same stretch of road on 6 March, 1980. The main witness was an archaeologist (now a retired county archaeologist), only slightly acquainted with the DPT, who has asked for anonymity. He had dropped by to visit one of the monitors at the King's Men circle. Afterwards, he returned to his vehicle, a large van, parked in the smaller of the two lay-bys near the circle. It was 1.45 pm. Sitting in the driver's cab, taking a bite of a sandwich, he suddenly saw "the back of a dog pass the [passenger] window from left to right – it was dark grey and short-haired, and I didn't see its head". The creature did not emerge in front of the van, so he opened the door of the vehicle and looked out, "but there was nothing to be seen". The archaeologist added: "On reflection, there seems no reason for me to call the object a dog, but I was convinced *immediately* ... that it was." (Personal communication, 11 March, 1980).

I further questioned this witness, and apart from the inexplicable disappearance of the creature, whatever it was, it became clear that in order for its back to have been seen above the bottom of the van window it must have stood about 1.2m (4ft) tall at the shoulder.

The third case that was reported to me as occurring along this specific length of road happened on 25 October, 1981. After a period of monitoring activity in the King's Men circle, a volunteer, Caroline Wise, took a break and strolled absent-mindedly along the road where it comes closest to the King's Men circle, and in the middle of the radioactive stretch:

I glanced down at the road surface and watched it [seemingly] form into a pattern of concentric circles about seven inches in diameter. Simultaneously, I felt like I was vibrating ... inside my head. It was like a 'buzzing' ... I was looking at the circles, and ... the road instantly returned to how it [normally] looked before. I looked up and saw an old-fashioned gypsy caravan; it was [made from] green wood and was the horse-drawn type. I saw it from behind. It was going away from us but hadn't passed us ... I glanced away, and when I looked back, the caravan had vanished. This whole incident lasted only a few seconds .... (Personal communication, 1987)

Old-style gypsy caravans would certainly have travelled along this road, the old ridgeway, in bygone times.

Another odd experience seemingly associated with that stretch of road was kindly brought to my attention by the celebrated Shakespearean and movie actor, (the now Sir) Mark Rylance. He and his wife Claire had founded their theatre company, Phoebus Cart, in 1990. Shortly thereafter, they took the company on tour performing at various adventurous locations, including the King's Men stone circle, where they put on Shakespeare's *The Tempest* "to draw as large a crowd as we could inside the circle ... to see what energy it created for them and us." The company lived across the road in tents and vans for two periods of a few weeks each, so they had an exceptionally extended and intimate relationship with the site. Rylance recalls that some of the company experienced short-term memory loss as they stayed longer in and around the circle. He goes on:

Claire had a particularly bad short-term memory loss when a particularly low black cloud appeared over the circle during a performance. She was playing a musical instrument on the eastern side of the circle and had to pass around the North of the circle, on the road, exchanging her instrument for another and then moving to the West side of the circle. She found herself in position in the West, with the new instrument but could not remember how she had got there or picked up the instrument.

Claire does not ever normally experience these kinds of short-term memory losses. Others had some experience of this as well, and she remembers it occurring more when one moved around the North of the circle, on the road. (Rylance 2019, personal communication)

We cannot definitively ascribe the heightened background radiation to the causation of any of these experiences, but one can stretch coincidence only so far. This is emphasised by the occurrence of recorded instances of these apparent altered mind-states (or are they time-slips, or dimensional portals?) associated with places of slightly raised radiation backgrounds elsewhere. Such as in the site examples below.

Site Examples

Boleigh Fogou, Cornwall, United Kingdom.

This site is located in the grounds of Rosemerryn House, near Lamorna, south of Penzance in Cornwall. It is an Iron Age souterrain, a class of subterranean megalithic structure referred to as *fogou* in Cornwall, a name derived from the Cornish for 'cave'. It is built from granite, and thus forms an enclosure that

Figure 26. Entrance to Boleigh Fogou

has an internal radiation level higher than background. Souter-rains also occur in Ireland, north-east Scotland, Brittany and the Orkney islands off Scotland's northern coast. Most if not all of the Scottish examples occur in granitic areas, as is the case in Brittany, while uranium has been found in Orkney's streams.

No one knows the purpose of the Cornish fogous. Some suggest they may have been hideaways from marauders, others posit that they were storage places for vegetables, while some feel they were places of ritual. All of the suggestions have their own pros and cons. But there is no doubt about the heightened radiation levels of the interiors of those measured, including Boleigh, where episodes of altered mind states have been reported.

One such report (passed on to me by the kind intervention of Cheryl Straffon, editor of the Cornish journal, *Meyn Mamvro*) involves a woman (who seeks anonymity) who spent time alone in the fogou at night:

As I stood there in the dark, I began to feel strangely without identity or time ... Suddenly it was no longer dark but I appeared to be standing in daylight a little way away from a church and watching a wedding party coming out of the church. The bride, groom and guests were there although I could not see faces clearly. It was a bit like watching a video in the clarity of the picture. Then I remember being distracted and feeling cold and the vision disappeared and went out. This was a bizarre experience – you could say that I must have dozed off and dreamt it, but for me the clarity and lucidity of the images made it different from a dream. In any case, I was vertical the whole time and I remember thinking to myself, "Well, how odd this is!'

If in prehistory such visionary/hallucinatory effects were first noted near granite outcrops and other sources of localized environmental radioactivity, the stone could in many societies have come to be used in later structures designed to augment ritual practices.

The King's Chamber, The Great Pyramid, Egypt

We have possible hints of this in ancient Egypt, inside the Great Pyramid. Too much has been written about the claimed mysteries of this huge monument to attempt even a synopsis here. What can be simply stated about it is that it does seem to encode fundamental, canonical measurements and ratios, though some claims as to what is supposed to be contained in the Great Pyramid's structure do enter the realm of 'pyramidiocy', to use the term coined by the late Glyn Daniel.

Figure 27. The Cheops Great Pyramid, Giza. [Photo: Nina Aldin Thune/ Wikimedia Commons/CC-BY-SA 2.5]

Access to the King's Chamber, positioned high up within the Pyramid, is initially by means of a very steep passage, the 'Grand Gallery', that inclines for 48m (157ft) up to the King's Chamber. This passage is of breathtaking exactitude, with polished stone surfaces. As John Anthony West correctly observes (1985): "It is difficult to avoid the impression that you are in the inside of an enormous instrument of some sort". Whatever else is true or false that is said about the Great Pyramid, there can be no doubt about the superb engineering of the architecture of this Old Kingdom edifice.

The Pyramid as a whole is built from limestone, but the King's Chamber is constructed from Aswan granite, quarried 965km (600 miles) away to the south. Granite was 'spirit stone' to the ancient Egyptians. The walls of the King's Chamber are made of exactly 100 granite blocks fitted together with utter precision. The floor is granite. The roof is formed by nine granite slabs, some

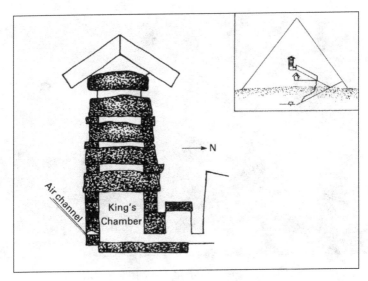

Figure 28. Elevation diagram of the King's Chamber in the Great Pyramid.

Figure 29. The granite, lidless sarcophagus inside the King's Chamber in the Great Pyramid.

weighing over 50 tonnes. Out of sight above that ceiling is a series of rough granite blocks ascending one above another, with air spaces between them.

The walls of the King's Chamber (and the entrance passages) are devoid of any inscriptions. At the west end of the chamber is a slightly damaged granite sarcophagus without a lid. It is too big to have been brought through the entrance passage. It is empty, with a plain exterior. To the modern archaeologist it has been robbed; to the esotericist it was used for initiatory practice and never had a mummy or grave goods within it. And what tomb robber would bother to struggle away with the lid of the sarcophagus?

To stand alone within the chamber is an awesome, profoundly eerie experience. It is a dark and sombre place. I took radiation measurements of the granite walls. The readings were of course higher than the desert background outside. Surprisingly, the readings for the interior of the sarcophagus, granite within granite, were the same as for the walls' surfaces. The biggest

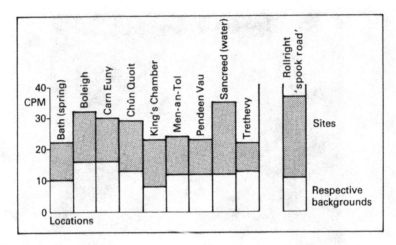

Figure 30: Histogram showing actual comparisons of radiation levels in counts per minute (CPM) at certain sites, including inside the King's Chamber and at the segment of Rollright 'spook road' where monitoring with the same instrument has taken place, along with their respective background readings. See text for further discussion.

surprise was that the *air count* in the middle of the chamber was substantially higher than the granite surfaces themselves – 36 percent higher on the day I monitored it. This was presumably due to radon seeping out of the granite on every side and simply accumulating within the chamber. The readings were similar to those obtained in some of the Cornish stone chambers.

For what it might be worth, I have no doubt in my own mind that this radiation-spiced air was intended to be breathed. The chamber has two narrow ducts leading from it – one inference can be that the chamber was meant to be used by the living. (Another suggestion is that it was to allow the pharaoh's soul to exit the chamber and ascend to the stars). And if that was the case, then the place must have been for psychospiritual activities. The radon atmosphere would have been one element used to help induce certain mental states. In his 1935 book, *A Search in Secret*

Egypt, Paul Brunton described an out-of-body experience he had when he spent the night alone in the chamber, for example.

The histogram in Figure 30 shows (shaded upper line) the comparative levels of radiation obtained by the same instrument at a range of sites, including the King's Chamber. The lower line shows the background environmental readings for the same places. The instrument's manufacturers say that normal, average background readings with the device will be about 12 cpm; in the figure, the total average of background radiation near the sacred sites is in fact 12.4 cpm. The sites themselves average 26.6 cpm. We can see from the histogram that sites individually range between two and three times higher than their local environments.

Bath (Aquae Sulis), England

The Roman baths and ruined temples which overlay the prehistoric sacred springs are enclosed within a museum-display precinct in the centre of Bath, close to the abbey. Bath is said to have Britain's only hot springs. They were resorted to at least 7,000 years ago, and in the Iron Age they were dedicated to the Celtic goddess, Sulis.

The Romans were strongly drawn to what was clearly a long venerated major Celtic shrine. They identified Sulis with one of their own goddesses, Minerva, but maintained the presence of the Celtic deity rather than supplanting her. They built a temple, bathing, and theatre complex at the springs. One of the many statues of the religious centre is known to have been dedicated to Sulis by a *haruspex* (diviner of the old Etruscan tradition) called Lucius Marcius Memor (Scullard 1979). A pediment above the entrance to the Sulis-Minerva temple depicted a so-called 'Gorgon's head'. Though this impressive, Celtic-style stone effigy

Figure 31. The Roman Great Bath at Bath, Somerset.

does have writhing hair, it also has an ample moustache – an unusual attribute for a goddess! Jacquetta Hawkes felt that it more likely represented the Celtic sun-god, with flames rather than snakes as a hairpiece, and added "in looking at what is certainly the finest example of the monumental sculpture of the Roman-ized Britons, we are seeing a creation which expresses something of the spirit, of the imaginative vision of the ancestral Celts, of ... prehistoric Britain" (Hawkes 1973). Roman walling enclosed Aquae Sulis, but as archaeologist Barry Cunliffe has noted, the area "is very much smaller than Roman country towns ... and suggests that the wall, rather than being a city wall may have been a temenos boundary defining the religious area" (Cunliffe 1985). Although on the fringes of the Roman Empire, Aquae Sulis was clearly a sacred site of some significance.

Figure 32. The so-called 'Gorgon's head' found at Aquae Sulis. See text.
[Author's drawing]

Detailed geological surveys have now discovered that the waters originated with ancient rain falling on the Mendip Hills which then seeped deep into the carboniferous limestone to be warmed by the natural heat emerging from the Earth's core at something between 64-96° C. From there the water flows along a major thrust fault forming an aquifer which allows some of the water to spread laterally beneath the impervious shales, marls and clays that form the floor of the valley at Bath. Under tremendous pressure, the waters rise to the surface where the strata are faulted and one of these, known as the Penny Quick Fault, passes through Bath. It is through fissures in this that the thermal waters ascend

Figure 33. Hot spring water overflowing from the reservoir at Bath through a Roman arch.

to become the hot springs of Bath, emerging in three places: the King's Spring (46.5° C); the Hetling Spring of the Old Royal Bath (49° C), and at the Cross Bath Spring (40° C). The waters are rich in some forty-three minerals including iron, magnesium, copper and potassium. And they are also radioactive.

In 1903, R.W. Strutt found "appreciable amounts" of radium in iron deposits left by the hot springs; the presence of radium in the water was confirmed by Nobel laureate, Sir William Ramsey (Williams and Stoddart 1978). I have monitored the main spring water with floating geiger counters and found it to have high natural radioactivity (relative to background levels), very much in keeping with levels found at a variety of sacred sites elsewhere, as Figure 30 shows.

Focus areas?

Megalithic monuments and some other anciently constructed sacred places do show a tendency to cluster, often in areas with heightened background radiation. Typically, granitic areas. Two classic examples that spring to mind are Dartmoor and Brittany, France.

We have already mentioned the 'salubrity' of Dartmoor's megalith-punctuated granite upland, but one of the world's greatest megalithic complexes, Carnac, is found in granitic Brittany. The French writer, Marc Dem, further notes that "France is the fourth most important producer of uranium in the West. The areas of France with the highest megalithic density correspond with uranium-rich zones." In Britain, where there is little uranium, he claims that "megalithic areas correspond with extensive but weak uranium deposits" and areas of "many anomalies" (Dem 1977).

Figure 34. The Kerlescan alignment of megaliths, part of the great Carnac megalithic complex, Brittany, France. [Photo: Myrabella/Wikimedia Commons/CC BY-SA 3.0 & GFDL]

In the context of possible focus areas, it may also be worth noting in passing an observation by the late Swiss researcher, Blanche Mertz. She remarked that some of the great Tibetan monasteries are in areas of "higher than normal radioactivity", and she measured high counts at numerous temples, such as that of Lakham Soma at Alchi. "The power points of monasteries are situated on the granite in this zone, and the builders certainly chose their sites in relation to the play of natural forces," Mertz reckoned (1987).

It could all be coincidental, but in the context of this book, one has to wonder.

2

MAGNETISM

Many kinds of rock contain sufficient quantities of such iron-bearing minerals as magnetite to display a measurable magnetism induced in them by the Earth's present-day magnetic field – which currently is about 0.47 gauss or 47,000 nT (nanoTesla). Common igneous rocks, such as basalt or granite, tend to show considerably higher magnetic susceptibilities than sedimentary rocks. But this induced magnetism may be only part of the total magnetism trapped in the rock. (Basalts, for instance, are significantly magnetic in their own right.) As iron minerals solidify from the molten magma, they become magnetized when the rock cools beneath a certain critical temperature known as the Curie Point. This 'fossil' or *remanent* magnetism provides a fingerprint of the magnetic fields of past geological ages. By looking back at the magnetic record held in rocks (palaeomagnetism), geologists have been able to learn that the geomagnetic field has reversed itself at various irregular intervals. The cause and implications of such reversals are not clearly understood at present.

Rocks with such complex magnetic histories can cause quite startling effects on the magnetized needles of compasses, and we will see how these more dramatic examples of 'magnetic stones' can sometimes be found occurring at natural places that have been identified as sacred, or actually incorporated into ancient structures.

MEASURING MAGNETISM IN THE PAST AND NOW

The first instrument used for detecting magnetism was the lodestone, a shaped piece of the strongly magnetic mineral magnetite, often with mineral impurities. The Earth's geomagnetic field is too weak to strongly magnetise magnetite on its own, but one theory is that lodestones are pieces of magnetite that have been magnetised by the magnetic fields accompanying lightning bolts.

If suspended from a cord, a lodestone can rotate to indicate the direction of the geomagnetic field, so was used for navigation (the original meaning of 'lode' was 'journey'). It is sometimes claimed that the earliest mention of lodestone was in Chinese literature – for example, the 4th-century B.C. *Book of the Devil Valley Master*. An earlier reference to lodestone's magnetic properties was made by the 6th-century B.C. Greek philosopher Thales of Miletus. But what appears to be the earliest archaeological evidence we have for the use of lodestone is in the rather mysterious Olmec culture (c.1200- 400 B.C.) of pre-Columbian Mexico (Devereux 2002). In 1975, astronomer John Carlson discovered a shaped and grooved magnetic bar at the Olmec site of San Lorenzo on Mexico's Gulf coast. It was found in strata dated between 1400 -1000 B.C. If allowed to float freely, the bar aligns its long axis 35 ° west of magnetic North (Evans 1977). Detailed analysis of the Olmec artifact revealed that it was actually composed of hematite with titanium, not magnetite, which accounted for its anomalous remanent magnetism. Carlson speculates that the Olmecs may have used the lodestone for astrological or architectural/geomantic purposes – he noted that there is a "family of Olmec site alignments eight degrees west of north [which] is a curiosity in its own right", and "the possibility that these alignments have an astronomical or geomagnetic origin should be explored" (Carlson 1975).

Modern instruments normally used to measure the magnitude or direction of the geomagnetic field are magnetometers. These come in a wide range of sensitivities and work to various principles. The two instruments owned by the Dragon Project, for instance, are of what is called the 'fluxgate' type and have a sensitivity down to around 15 nT and respond to movements in the magnetic field as well as field strength. As will be described below, unexplained variations of low-level magnetism within standing stones have been measured. The trouble with measuring at these low levels, however, is that all kinds of ambient variables in the environment can affect readings and have to be carefully guarded against.

It was the Carn Ingli (Preseli, South Wales) case (below) that alerted us to the fact that some magnetic effects at prehistoric places were of a kind able to register unambiguously on simple magnetic compasses, and that we need not always have to use magnetometers.

Orthodox archaeology uses magnetometers to locate areas of magnetic disturbance caused by the burial of iron objects, wall foundations, or places such as kilns or hearths where there has been intense heat and burning. In this way, a site being considered for excavation can be plotted for points of interest without the ground being physically disturbed, thus targeting future excavational activity more accurately.

SENSING MAGNETISM

So, people in antiquity could have gained knowledge of magnetism (however they envisaged that invisible force) by means of lodestones. But there may possibly have been another way – direct sensing. The formal term for that is 'magnetoreception'.

It is now known that a wide variety of creatures have varying sensitivities to geomagnetism. For instance, researchers have found that bacteria can respond to a magnet moved around them, and that snails and worms can detect incredibly weak magnetic fields. Larger creatures too: pigeons can navigate by the use of their sensitivity to the geomagnetic field in addition to other direction-finding aids, such as the position of the sun, while whales and dolphins seem able to cruise along 'magnetic stripes' laid out on the ocean floors due to tectonic action. Other creatures scientifically tested and found to possess magnetic sensitivity include algae, crabs, salmon, sharks, honey bees, fruit flies, salamanders, robins, mice, turtles, deer. And so on. The list of lifeforms known to be sensitive to subtle levels of magnetism is now very long.

It has been shown in experiments that some animals can detect magnetic levels below a thousandth of a gauss (remember the Earth's field strength is about half a gauss!). The sensitivity to magnetic change of the yellowfin tuna has been found to be in the order of 1nT (less than one twenty-thousandth of the Earth's field). In some cases, such as pigeons and certain bacteria, the magnetoreceptor appears to be minute particles of magnetite or iron sulphide ('magnetosomes') embedded in the creature's body. It is as if these organisms are carrying their own biological lodestone. In some cases, though, the precise nature and location of the magnetic receptor remains elusive.

If other organisms can detect magnetism, what about human beings? Researcher Michael Shallis found that profoundly electrically sensitive people tend to suffer from allergies which may have an electrical basis. One of Shallis' subjects was not only phenomenally responsive to electrical fields, but also to magnetism:

When he is ill from his allergies, he finds the telephone helps him to recover: he says the magnet in the earpiece seems to stabilise his immune system. More dramatic is his sensitivity to the Earth's magnetic field: when his allergy reactions debilitate him, he becomes acutely aware of direction. If he faces north, he feels better and rather euphoric. Facing or moving south makes his symptoms worse and can even provoke unconsciousness. East-west directions seem neutral to him. As he lives north of the allergy clinic, travelling southwards to it is a hazardous journey for him and he can pass out en route. There have been times when he has had to be taken to the clinic by a circuitous route, tacking eastwards and westwards, rather like a yacht against the wind, in order to minimise the southward passage of his movement. (Shallis 1988)

Yves Rocard, who was a physics professor at the Ecole Normale in Paris, similarly showed that human beings can detect magnetic changes down to 10^{-8} gauss. Dr. Robin Baker, formerly of the Department of Zoology at Manchester University, thinks human magnetic sensitivity probably does exist (Baker 1989). By the early 1980s, Baker and his team had detected a thin embedded layer of high-iron content in the bones forming the walls of the sinuses, which is in close proximity to parts of the brain. But even with this magnetic centre, human beings would need to train themselves to use it readily.

The idea of human magnetic sensitivity is still controversial, but experiments continue. In 2011, for instance, scientists announced that a protein in the human eye does display magnetic sensitivity (Foley et al. 2011). There has even been informed speculation that biological sensitivity to the geomagnetic field has helped shape human evolution (Ivanhoe 1979).

More recent supporting evidence comes from researchers in the United States and Japan (Wang et al. 2019). They placed thirty-four participants individually inside a six-sided cage, the walls of which were made of aluminium to shield against electromagnetic interference. The walls also contained coils through which currents were passed to mimic the geomagnetic field. Inside the cage each participant was asked to sit still on a wooden chair in the dark, facing straight ahead towards the north. During the experiment, the team measured the participant's brain waves using an electroencephalogram (EEG). The applied magnetic fields were fixed in one direction, while some others were rotated. In yet others the machines were turned on but no magnetic field was produced, so that the participant was only exposed to Earth's natural magnetic field. Of course, the participant was unaware which variations were under way at any given time. The collective results of the experiments showed that various configurations of the generated magnetic fields produced changes in participants' alpha brain waves, which are associated with the brain's information processing. This would allow a person to register an unexpected change in their geomagnetic environment. (The researchers remark that the strength of the response varied markedly among participants.) The research team point out that these results might offer indications as to what the human magnetoreception system might look like. "We have not as a species lost the magnetic sensory system that our ancestors had," said Professor Joseph Kirschvink, one of the research team. "We are part of Earth's magnetic biosphere." Indeed.

So, there is some evidence of at least potential human awareness of subtle changes in geomagnetic fields. One wonders if this sensibility was more marked in people of the Stone Age, when, incidentally, the Earth's field may have been stronger, and when the world was much quieter in electro-magnetic terms, without the all-pervading maelstrom of today's technological develop-ments – a factor that may, in fact, have caused us to progressively shut down such sensitivity.

MAGNETISM IN ANCIENT HEALING AND MAGIC

One can romp through a range of claims regarding magnetism and healing, some perhaps better founded or more relevant than others. Modern medicine uses pulsed low-frequency magnetic fields to treat bone fractures (and folklore tells us that bone disor-ders were one of the chief ailments brought to the standing stones for treatment), and some forms of alternative medicine today use the application of magnets to treat certain disorders. In Japan, for instance, they are thought to help arthritis and rheumatism, and the Russians use water exposed to magnetism to ease painful urination. There are claims of magnetic fields inhibiting the spread of tumours. Folklore from the earliest times tells of the healing properties of magnets and the lodestone. There are references in early Vedic scripts to the use of the magnet for stopping bleeding; in Egypt, it is said that Cleopatra wore a lodestone amulet, and there are references to the therapeutic use of magnets from the ancient Greeks through to the Middle Ages. And Pliny the Elder acknowledged that the Egyptians knew about magnetism. He relates that the architect for the temple of the Ptolemaic Egyptian queen Arsinoe IV (died 41 B.C.) "had begun to use lodestone for constructing the vaulting in the Temple of Arsinoe at Alexandria, so that the iron statue contained in it might have the appearance of being suspended in mid-air; but the project was interrupted by his own death and that of King Ptolemy who had ordered the work to be done in honour of his sister." (Pliny, Natural History, XLII)

MAGNETISM AND THE MIND

It is known that the temporal-lobe area of the brain is sensitive to electro-magnetism; it is a brain region containing the hippocampus, which is functionally related to dreaming and to memory. The late Professor Michael Persinger of Laurentian University and his teams and associates have made considerable study of this, and low-level magnetic stimulation of these brain regions seems able to produce in the subject sensations of floating, including out-of-body sensations, the intrusion of vivid hallucinatory images into waking consciousness, and even mystical and visionary states. Persinger and colleagues have produced some exciting if controversial statistical evidence that suggests that there is a link between some forms of psi (extra-sensory) activity in humans and the activity of the geomagnetic field (e.g. Persinger and Schaut 1988).

Persinger is famous (or infamous) for his so-called "God helmet", a helmet that holds electrodes in place on the wearer's temples that generate programmed patterns of weak magnetic fields which massage the temporal cortex producing sensations of unseen "presences" and other strange perceptions and altered mind states. (In fact, the reason Persinger had initially developed this procedure was to explore the neurological use of magnetism in therapy in place of pharmaceutical products.) I have myself undergone a session with the helmet under Persinger's direction, and in my case, I saw glowing phosphenes (light phenomena generated from within the eye) take on three-dimensional, sculptural form and tumble away into a spatially vast empty void.

On the heels of this device, Persinger and colleagues developed a further instrument, nicknamed "the octopus" on account of all the wires involved in the prototype. More properly known

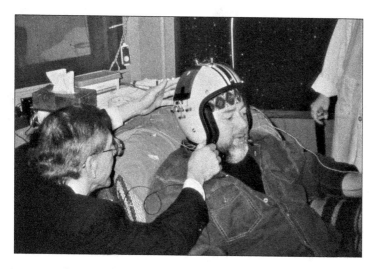

Figure 35. The author being prepared by the late Professor Michael Persinger for a session with the so-called 'God Helmet'. [Photo: Charla Devereux.]

as a circumcerebral magnetic stimulation (CMS) device, this, basically, is comprised of solenoids (coils) set at intervals on a headband fitted around a person's cranium. The solenoids are controlled by a computer program that enables them to rotate precisely-configured weak magnetic pulses around the head. This magnetic stimulation can affect the brain in certain ways, including partially disrupting the 40 Hz so-called "binding factor" of the brain which normally seems to help pull all our sensory inputs together into a smooth, seamless perception of the world. Put in non-technical language, this disruption allows normally curtailed or filtered information from what Aldous Huxley (1959) referred to as "Mind-at-Large" to reach awareness. Some of this information can seemingly possess psi properties, whatever they turn out to be. I have been a fan of this CMS device ever since I tried out a prototype at Laurentian. It gave me a totally unambiguous, veridical remote perception experience.

SITE EXAMPLES

The King's Men stone circle, Rollright Stones, England

As already noted, this site was the main field headquarters of the Dragon Project for some of its earlier years. Initially, the Project did not have the resources for purchasing magnetometers, and universities were not keen on loaning out equipment to a strange, in their perception possibly wacky outfit conducting work at remote places in tough, outdoor conditions. As such, study of environmental magnetism languished within the DPT quite some time, and so no serious on-site magnetic study was conducted until 1983. Then, in January of that year, an article appeared in *New Scientist*. Charles Brooker, a retired BBC engineer and horticultural engineering consultant, had conducted a magnetic survey of Rollright's King's Men circle as part of a set of investigations he was pursuing privately. He used the stone circle only because it was the nearest suitable site for his purposes to where he hired his equipment. Brooker appeared to have made some discoveries during the course of his work that were relevant to the Dragon Project's interests. He claimed to have re-checked his findings with a second, more sensitive, instrument before publishing his brief report in *New Scientist*. "The average intensity of the [geomagnetic] field within the circle was significantly lower than that measured outside, as if the stones acted as a shield," he wrote (1983).

We got in contact with Brooker and learnt that he had also discovered something else that in some ways was even more interesting – he had measured two stones, on the western side of the circle, which were magnetically pulsing. They gave a cyclic variation of 50-60 gamma at a frequency of 40-60 seconds. This seemed the most suitable effect reported by Brooker for us to check ourselves, and we resolved to get access to a magnetometer. Eventually, we obtained a flux-gate type machine with Hall probe on weekend loan from Birkbeck College, London, and, on 3 July 1983, a DPT team assembled at the King's Men. The Project's main electronics expert, Rodney Hale, operated the equipment; along with a few regular Project volunteers, and myself, there were also a geologist and a physicist present to observe. The magnetometer was old and unwieldy, but it offered us our first opportunity to obtain direct magnetic measurements. Units for various types of magnetic measurement include the oersted, gauss, gamma, and tesla. Here, we were measuring in millioersteds (mOe).

A horizontal line at O on the four graphs in Figure 37 represent the Earth's field, and we were seeing falls below that value (hence the mOe values are shown with a minus sign in front of them).

Figure 36. Rodney Hale, a key Dragon Project investigator, tests the functioning of a magnetometer inside the King's Men stone circle, in preparation for using it to measure some of the stones themselves. Geologist Paul McCartney (right) looks on. A marked anomaly was found in one of the stones, see text.

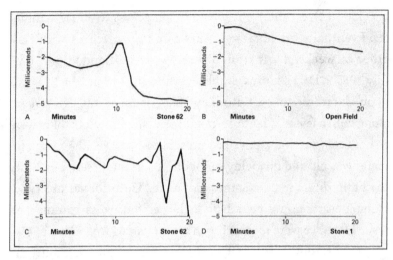

Figure 37 a,b,c,d. Graphs showing magnetometer findings at two stones in the King's Men circle and one control site over 3km (2 miles) distant. See text.

The weather was warm and dry. We chose Stone 62 (Barnatt survey) in the north-west quadrant of the circle for the first 20-minute monitoring session. As the minutes went by, we could see from the magnetometer's meter that there was some fluctuation going on. Changes between O and -3 could be accounted for by variations of temperature within the internal circuitry of the instrument, but towards the end of the period there were slightly larger shifts. We next went to an open field site about 3km (2 miles) from the circle to conduct a control set of measurements (Figure 37b). Here the graph shows a steady drift within the range of the instrument's internal circuitry variations. We returned to Stone 62 and hooked it up for another 20-minute session (Figure 37c). After ten minutes, we could see the choppy nature of the changes, but they were still within the bounds of instrumental 'noise'. But there was a big dip at 17 minutes followed by a peak. Then, almost at the end of the session, the readings began to drop and continued to do so until we had to change scale on the meter. At 23 minutes, we had a reading of -28 mOe. No one present could account for the sudden, significant change. There had been no observable variations in the environment of Stone 62. Everyone was kept well away from the megalith; there were no cars or aircraft passing by during the monitoring period. We then measured the tallest stone in the circle (Stone 1, Barnatt survey), which is nearest to the road: Figure 37d shows a perfect reading without any anomalies. A stone on the southern side of the circle (Stone 37, Barnatt survey), also gave a smooth, normal graph. Before we left the site that day, we measured Stone 62 again. It gave a level, anomaly-free reading. Stone 62 was not one of those monitored by Brooker, so the two separate studies had shown three Rollright stones varying magnetically on the days the respective surveys took place. We did not know the cause, and we still do not.

By early 1987, the Dragon Project had two of its own magnetometers, courtesy of Hale's electronic engineering workshop, and these have been used at many sites and their environments in Britain and Brittany. Hale and helpers also conducted many trials with the new equipment at the King's Men circle during the course of 1987. By September of that year, the cautious Hale felt he could state that "there seems to be some evidence growing of a fluctuating field within the circle relative to outside, changing over a period of hours." This, of course, echoes Brooker's tentative conclusion.

More and longer-term research like this is still crying out to be conducted these many years after this Dragon Project pilot study.

Carn Ingli, Mynedd Preseli, South Wales, United Kingdom

Carn Ingli is one of the westernmost peaks of Mynedd Preseli (the Preseli Hills), overlooking the small town of Newport on the west coast of Wales. The Preseli Hills possesses a remarkable atmosphere – wild, rugged and with a pervading sense of remoteness from the present day, and they were like a magnet to prehistoric people, evidenced by remarkable monuments dating from before even the Neolithic period through to the Iron Age, scattered on and around them.

As we shall explore in more detail later on, geologists have found that the bluestones of far-away Stonehenge originated from various 'carns' – jagged outcrops of igneous rocks – that stand out starkly along the ridges of the hills. Carn Ingli is one of the most spectacular of these rugged peaks, around which people long ago

Figure 38. The Pentre Ifan dolmen with Carn Ingli in background

draped necklaces of stone, now tumbled rock walls that today mingle with its crags almost as natural extensions. 'Carn Ingli' can be translated as 'The Hill of Angels'. It got this name because of a 6th-century Irish anchorite, St Brynach, who was a friend and contemporary of St David, the patron saint of Wales. Brynach founded a number of churches, most important among them the one at Nevern, a hamlet tucked away in remote country just north of Mynedd Preseli. The church enclosure has an almost palpable sense of the sacred about it and has a 'bleeding yew', which exudes resin like a sticky, blood-red wound from its trunk, as well as a remarkable Saxon cross. From immediately outside the church-yard there is a clear view of Carn Ingli, and it was to this peak that the saint repaired periodically to conduct prayerful meditation, in which it is said he was able to communicate with the angels.

Carn Ingli took on significance from a 'site-energy' point of view due to an incident that was reported early in 1987 to 'Llowarch ', the pen-name of Keith Stevenson, a then column-ist for the Cambrian News: a young man and his girlfriend were driving near Carn Ingli when the woman complained of curious sensations, as if she was being subjected to waves of some kind of force that seemed to be originating from the peak itself. The couple parked their car and approached Carn Ingli on foot, but the closer they got, the more strongly the girl felt the sensations. Becoming concerned, they retreated to the car and left the area. The young man told his father, a local man, about the odd experi-ence, and that is how Stevenson first got to hear of the affair. In May 1987, Stevenson was able to visit the place for himself, and during investigation of the craggy height he noted strong compass anomalies at points amongst the rocks. Stevenson contacted me about the matter, and later in the summer of 1987 I visited Carn Ingli. I was certainly able to confirm the magnetic anomalies.

The compass needle moved tens of degrees off magnetic north in some places, while in a few it turned full south – a deflection of 180 degrees. This could be obtained just by holding the compass in mid-air at certain points. We conducted compass checks at several other Preseli rock outcrops, but nothing remotely comparable to the effects at Carn Ingli were discovered.

Bearing in mind the magnetic sensitivity of the temporal cortex discussed above, was this field anomaly the secret of the place, causing it to be picked by a Dark Ages holy man as a place where he learned that he could more readily enter altered mind states and experience visions?

I mentioned the phenomenon some time afterwards to an inspector of Heritage England (the body responsible for the care of ancient monuments in England) when we both happened to be in the Preseli area. He was duly impressed when he accompanied me to the site and saw the compass response. He later informed me that he had visited Carn Ingli again, in the company of two women. One of these suddenly complained of hearing sounds that seemed inexplicable under normal circumstances. All three of them, he told me, saw a rainbow effect in the sky over the peak. "That was at least symbolic," I suggested. The inspector replied that it was more than that: "At the time we saw it, darkness had fallen!" (My informant didn't state if the moon was bright that evening – 'moonbows' are possible.) In addition, we later heard, quite separately, that local people had reported disembodied voices on the slopes of Carn Ingli, and also the sound of marching feet, with nobody visible. In fact, all these are consistent with auditory hallucinatory effects caused by disturbed magnetic field environments and have been noted elsewhere in connection with light phenomena (Devereux 1989) and powerful northern lights (Grant 1984).

Carnac, Brittany, France

At the greatest megalithic complex of them all, around Carnac-Ville in Brittany, Belgian researcher Pierre Mereaux has found an interesting magnetic correlation. The most famous of the Carnac area's thousands of megaliths are the great multiple rows of standing stones forming several groups of alignments. Mereaux took 240 magnetic readings with a sensitive instrument. He reported:

> The whole area included between the alignments, from the west of Erdeven to the northeast of Carnac, shows a very stable magnetic field, with slight negative or positive variations in the order of 10 gammas. The alignments proper form a precise frontier to this zone, and the field begins to be disturbed in the middle of the field of menhirs, where the variations already reach 200 to 250 gammas. At Kermario, Kerlescan and at Le Menec, to the south of the alignments, outside the zone studied, the disturbances vary between -400 and +1100 gammas. The only exception concerns the rows of standing stones of Kerkerho at Erdeven, where the stable magnetic field passes slightly outside of the rows of menhirs, next to the two great stones standing to the north of the alignment.

Even while staying within the cautious limits of a certain scientific rigour, this would seem to demonstrate that the fields of menhirs of this area were not planted there by chance and that their presence would be in direct relation to terrestrial magnetism ... This may be summarised by a double question: 'Were the menhirs raised there because of the curious characteristics of the place, or does the place have curious characteristics because of the presence of the menhirs?'(Mereaux 1981)

The 'Nazca Lines', Peru

On the pampa near Nazca, Peru, are the famous 'Nazca lines': hundreds of dead straight lines covering the desert surface. No one truly knows who marked them on the desert pavement nor what their purpose could possibly have been (though see Devereux 2010). They were probably produced during the first millennium A.D. Sprinkled amongst the lines are older, giant drawings of creatures, spirals, and abstract designs. The late Maria Reiche, a German mathematician, dedicated half her life to the study of the lines. She was by no means a woman given to thoughtless frivolity (I met her), so her brief comments on unusual phenomena amidst the lines, recorded in Tony Morrison's *The Mystery of the Nasca Lines* (1987), carry particular weight. "There is one place on the pampa which is very strange," Reiche stated. "I found it when I was measuring ... No, perhaps I'd better not say where it is, but anyway that doesn't matter too much – it's a place where the compass doesn't work. The needle stops at any point on the dial and you lose yourself very easily ... someone once said it could be caused by a large piece of buried metal. (Maria Reiche also noted mysterious moving lights on the desert.)

The 'Stones of Acq', France

Blanche Mertz found three magnetic anomalies at these megaliths near the village of Ecoivres, in the Pas-de-Calais. One stone is over 2.5m (8ft) tall and its companion rises to slightly more than 3.10m (10ft). They form a north-west-south-east alignment, with one magnetic-anomaly spot lying between them, another immediately to their north, and a third just to their west.

Mount Tamalpais, California

There is a serpentine outcrop containing areas of magnetic anomaly on the upper slopes of this mountain, which overlooks San Francisco Bay. It forms a natural 'seat', and is, apparently, a Native American 'power centre'. Sitting there, the base of one's spine is kept comfortably but firmly erect against a magnetic anomaly spot, and with the rest of one's body in a different magnetic field. It is feasible (I put it no stronger than that) that this might stimulate what Hindus call 'kundalini' energy, the same spiritual charge up the spine produced by San Bushmen in southern Africa during their trance dances. One can perhaps envisage a pre-Columbian shaman, after dancing and chanting himself into a trance, maybe with a little help from a psychoactive

Figure 39. Serpentine outcrop on Mount Tamalpias, California.

Datura mixture (favoured by the ancient Chumash Indians in this region), seating himself against the magnetic stone for entry to the spirit world.

Monte Alto Culture, Guatemala

The 'Monte Alto' culture in Guatemala is thought to have preceded the Olmec culture, making it one of the oldest in the Americas. These peoples produced stone sculptures, many of which are magnetic. Of a collection of four so-called 'fat boy' or 'potbelly' sculptures, now on display in the town park of La Democracia, in front of its local museum, four of the heads and three of the bodies

Figure 40. A 'potbelly' sculpture from Monte Alto in the plaza at La Democracia, Escuintla, Guatemala. These types of sculptures were carved from boulders containing points of magnetism of which the sculptors seemed to be aware. See text. [Photo: Simon Burchell/Wikimedia Commons/CC BY-SA 3.0]

were found to have magnetic properties. All four of the heads have a north magnetic pole located in their right temples, while three of them have south magnetic poles below the right ear and the fourth (the one right in front of the museum) has a south magnetic pole in its left temple. This at least suggests the possibility of deliberate knowledge and use of the stones' magnetic properties by the sculptors, and others of their sculptures indicate the same thing. For example, one 'fat boy' has a magnetic pole at its navel, another depicts two men sitting cross-legged with arms crossed on their chests with north magnetic poles where they cross. Again, a sculpture of a rampant jaguar was found to have north magnetic poles in both of its paws, but no discernible south poles.

3

SEISMIC FAULTING AND ASSOCIATED PHENOMENA

There were a variety of pragmatic or mythological reasons that determined the placement of ancient sacred sites in the landscape, as already mentioned, but until recently there has been little consideration of geological factors, such as fault lines or associated geophysical effects. These fractures in the Earth's crust caused by seismic action not only can be sites of radiation and magnetic anomalies, but around these geological discontinuities are also various other phenomena, such as gaseous emissions, electrical effects associated with mineral enrichment around faulting, and the occasional occurrence of strange lights – as we shall see. Along with the obvious association of earthquakes with faulting, other related phenomena were, I suggest, other ways such locations could hold significance for ancient cultures.

SITE PLACEMENTS AND FAULTING

Before the commencement of the Dragon Project, there had been loose conjecture by 'ancient earth mysteries' enthusiasts, notably, John Michell, that megalithic sites were placed on geological faulting, but such assertions were not the result of any actual study. So, in the early days of the DPT, as already mentioned, we asked its geological consultant, Paul McCartney, to see if these rumours were accurate. From his study of the geology and megalithic distribution in England and Wales, McCartney found that only stone circles could be confidently associated with faulting in those countries: he was satisfied that every stone circle is within a mile of a surface fault or lies on an associated intrusion. Even in areas one would not initially associate with faulting, like that around the King's Men circle at the Rollright Stones in Oxfordshire, the pattern holds, as we have noted – the Rollright Fault runs about three-quarters of a mile away from the circle. This is the sort of pattern that is repeated throughout the country.

The pattern holds up at close quarters as well, even in Scotland, where McCartney did not do a full survey. The Isle of Lewis in the Outer Hebrides, off the west coast of Scotland, lies as a whole alongside the major Minch Fault, but if we look closely at

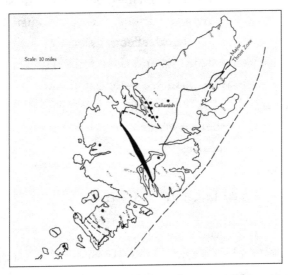

Figure 41. A geological sketch of the Isle of Lewis, in the Scottish Outer Hebrides. Dashed lines represent major faults, black circles stone circles, and the large black line represents a major anticlinal axis. The close correlation between faulting and the Callanish Stones group (marked) is evident. [After Paul McCartney]

Figure 42. Part of the main Callanish Stones complex on the Scottish Isle of Lewis. [Photo: Chmee2 (Petr Brož)/Wikimedia Commons/CC BY-SA 3.0)]

the relationship between faulting on the island and the stone circle group associated with the island's famous Callanish Complex, we can see how tight the correlation can be (Figure 41).

Archaeologists have tended to dismiss such site-fault placement patterns with a "so what?" shrug – they certainly did with these early observations – but now geologists, at least, have begun to note the possible significance of such associations. In a 2017 paper entitled "Seismic faults and sacred sanctuaries in Aegean antiquity", researchers Iain Stewart and Luigi Piccardi argue that earthquake faulting may have played a role in shaping the culture of ancient Greece. It is worth quoting their paper's Abstract in full, as it touches on many relevant aspects of faulting, such as springs, groundwater and gases and their cultural significance:

The ancient destructive capability of earthquake faults is well chronicled by historians and their cultural impact widely uncovered by archaeologists. Archaeological and geological investigations at some of the most renowned sites in the ancient Greek world however, suggest a more nuanced and intimate relationship between seismic faults and past human settlements. In the Aegean's karstic landscape earthquake fault scarps act as limestone ramparts on which fortifications, citadels and acropoli were constructed, and underlying fault lines were preferred pathways for groundwater movement and egress. The vital purifactory or therapeutic role of natural springs in the ritual practices of early settlements implies that the fault lines from which they leaked may have helped position the nascent hubs of Greek cities. Equally, the tendency for earthquakes to disrupt groundwater patterns and occasionally shut down persistent springs provides a hitherto unrecognised mechanism for the abrupt demise of those same settlements. Votive niches, carvings, reliefs and inscriptions on fault surfaces suggest important sacred sanctuaries, particularly those with oracular functions, may have been deliberately built astride active fault traces and venerated as direct connections to the chthonic realm ("the underworld"). Regionally, the Aegean's distributed network of tensional faulting, circulating geothermal waters and deep-seated degassing sets the tectonic framework for the springs and gases that infuse the ancient Greek netherworld of caves, chasms, chambers, and sacred grottos. The possibility that seismic faults may have constituted the fulcrum of prominent sacred places means that, for all their obvious destructiveness, earthquakes may have had an unacknowledged cultural significance in Greek antiquity. (Stewart and Piccardi 2017)

An example showing that the ancient Greeks deliberately adapted to earthquake conditions can be seen at the oracle temple of

Figure 43. The anti-seismic platform of the Temple of Apollo at Delphi.

Delphi, where the temple's platform is designated as 'anti-seismic' because it is built from irregularly-shaped and relatively loose-ly-packed rocks, allowing for tension-releasing movement without collapse during earthquakes (Figure 43).

And not only ancient Greece – the Andes holds similar ancient and sacred secrets. Machu Picchu, for example. This a 15th-century Inca citadel, located on a narrow Andean mountain ridge at an altitude of 2,430m (7,970ft), 80km (50 miles) north-west of Cuzco, Peru. Although known to local Andean Indians, it was not known to the Spanish during the colonial period and remained unknown to the outside world until American historian Hiram Bingham brought it to international attention in 1911. The site complex consists of three main structures or features, plus outlying buildings. Restoration of the citadel continues. It was declared a UNESCO World Heritage Site in 1983.

At a meeting of the Geological Society of America (GSA) held in Phoenix, September 2019, geologist Rualdo Menegat, from Brazil's Federal University of Rio Grande do Sul, presented

Figure 44. Machu Picchu, Peru. [Photo: Diego Delso (delso.photo)/
Wikimedia Commons/CC-BY-SA]

the results of a detailed geoarchaeological analysis that suggests
the Incas intentionally built Machu Picchu – as well as some of
their cities – in locations where tectonic faults converge. "Machu
Picchu's location is not a coincidence," Menegat asserts.

Using a combination of satellite imagery and field measurements, Menegat mapped a web of intersecting fractures and faults
beneath the citadel. He found that these faults and fractures occur
in several sets, some of which correspond to the major fault zones
responsible for uplifting the Central Andes Mountains. "Because
some of these faults are oriented northeast-southwest and others
trend northwest-southeast, they collectively create an 'X'-shape
where they intersect beneath Machu Picchu," the geologist states.

Menegat's mapping suggests that the sanctuary's urban
sectors and the surrounding agricultural fields, as well as individual buildings and stairs, are all oriented along the trends of these
major faults. "The layout clearly reflects the fracture matrix under-

lying the site," says Menegat. Other ancient Incan cities, including Ollantaytambo, Pisac, and Cuzco, are also located at the intersection of faults. "Each is precisely the expression of the main directions of the site's geological faults." (Menegat 2019)

This study indicates that the the fault network at Machu Picchu probably offered the Incas a ready source of water – the area's tectonic faults channelled meltwater and rainwater straight to the site, and also helped drain the site during the intense rainstorms to which the region is subject.

As if to reinforce this research, a different and slightly more recent study (October 2019) revealed that Machu Picchu suffered at least two strong earthquakes even while it was being built. (Rodríguez-Pascua et al. 2019)

Another way ancient peoples could have been aware of and used faulting is dramatically shown at the essentially Anasazi site of Wupatki, near Flagstaff in Arizona, close to the Sunset Crater volcano. The Anasazi culture reached its height between A.D. 900–1300 and collapsed in the 15th Century for reasons that are not entirely clear. It is thought the Anasazi were the forerunners of today's Pueblo peoples, such as the Hopi. Wupatki is a now ruined collection of adobe buildings, a 'pueblo', some of which were merged with naturally outcropping rock. It dates to A.D. 1100–1225, and is a mixture of Sinagua and Kayenta Anasazi Indian work. The buildings are positioned directly above cracks in the Kaibab limestone beneath them, and the Native American builders consciously incorporated seismic vents to allow for cyclic exhalations of air issuing from deep beneath the ground. These 'blowholes' are openings to an estimated seven billion cubic feet of subterranean caverns, fissures and faults. Factors such as changes in air pressure, thunderstorms and variations in surface temperature can affect the flow of air through these holes or vents,

Figure 45. The scarf is blowing upwards due to the powerful
gusts of air issuing vigorously from a blowhole at Wupatki.

but usually air is drawn into the blowholes during the night and
early morning, and out during the afternoon. Sometimes the air
exits the vents at up to 30 mph. In Figure 45, we can see from the
chiffon scarf that the blowhole is 'exhaling'. Some Hopi wind-god
legends refer to these blowholes, but we do not know fully what
they meant to the ancient people who lived at Wupatki.

SACRED WATERS

The ancient Greeks had hundreds of healing centres and temples
called 'Asclepeions' (various anglicised spellings), dedicated
to the healing god, Asclepius. Anyone seeking healing at an
Asclepeion would undergo a variety of spiritual and physical

purifications in which water figured prominently. Eventually, the person seeking healing would be given an infusion of herbs, possibly psychoactive or soporific in nature, and then enter a dream cell (*abaton*) and sleep on a stone bed, hoping Asclepius or a symbol representing him, would appear in a dream – a process now often referred to as 'temple sleep'. Assistants known as *therapeutes* would later interpret supplicants' dreams for them, advising on the course of treatment indicated by the dream imagery.

We will revisit all this in Chapter 6, but our interest right here is that most, if not all, Asclepeions were located at or near faulting, probably because of the associated water sources. Just for example, at Epidaurus, a major Asclepeion, there is a very ancient well beneath the building that housed the special cells where people went to have their healing dreams. Again, another

Figure 46. A statue in Berlin's Neu Museum depicting
Asclepius with his serpent-entwined staff.

Figure 47. The ruins of the building that contained the sleep cells (abatons) at the Asclepeion of Epidaurus, situated over a more ancient, venerated sacred well.

one at Corinth had nine reservoirs of crystal-clear water, as well as using water imported from a distant hot spring via a special road eleven miles long – the water from that source has been found to be radioactive.

It was not just the temples dedicated to Asclepius that were associated with fault-based water sources. At the famous oracle temple of Dodona, in northern Greece, a sacred spring gushed forth from beneath the root of a great oak that stood there and the murmurings of the emerging water were subject to oracular interpretation. Or, take the citadel of Mycenae as another example. It is perched on top of a rocky hill in the eastern Peloponnese region of mainland Greece and is built directly over an active fault. And it is home to a major sacred spring, which, though located just outside the citadel, "could be accessed from within the city walls via a subterranean passageway that tapped the fault zone," Iain Stewart (ibid.) tells us. Indeed, it seems it was this fault that ruptured during Mycenaean times causing widespread destruction of the citadel. And there are many more examples.

Now, there are many faults in the eastern Mediterranean and Aegean region – they are "endemic", as Stewart admits. So is it all chance? "I have always thought it more than coincidence that many important sites are located directly on top of fault lines created by seismic activity ... perhaps the building of temples and cities close to these sites was more systematic than has previously been thought," he argues. Quite so.

In any case, a similar pattern is found elsewhere in the world, outside the immediate ancient Greek sphere of influence, as we shall note in the Site Examples section below.

STRANGE LIGHTS

My own curiosity regarding the relationship between the Earth and lights was piqued in 1957, when I was a schoolboy in Leicestershire in central England. In that year and county there was

Figure 48. An abaton's stone couch still surviving at the Corinth Asclepeion.

a significant earthquake, in which I saw the school walls bulge
(but fortunately not collapse). A teacher who had taken a school
party out on a field trip to nearby Charnwood Forest – a dramatic, fault-ridden and ancient upland landscape where later Triassic
sediments sit directly on top of Precambrian rocks – stated that he
and the kids saw lines of "tadpole-shaped" lights crossing the sky
just before the quake struck. It was no accident, then, that many
years later a colleague and I chose to conduct an investigation
of reports spanning a few centuries telling of strange phenomena, including curious lights, in our home county. It formed a
two-part article entitled 'Portrait of a Fault Area' (Devereux and
York 1975). Although fairly primitive, this geographical study
nevertheless clearly indicated that over the centuries modern
'UFOs' (as the current fashion has it) and earlier "balls of light"
or "meteors" in Leicestershire shared a common distribution
with faulting, seismic activity and unusual meteorology.

One of the earliest modern investigators to raise awareness
of such 'earth lights' was the American, Charles Fort. In assem-
bling his compendious record of unusual events, Fort began to
spy possible connections that virtually no one before him had the
range of data or wit to perceive. He linked strange aerial lights
with earthquakes, predating modern geological confirmation of
'earthquake lights' (EQLs). For example, he drew attention to the
December 1896 earthquake in the Hereford - Worcester region of
Britain (Fort 1923). He found reports describing such effects as "a
great blaze" in the sky and a flying "luminous object" coincident
with the quake. Fort acidly commented that "the conventional
scientist" of his day had a "reluctance toward considering shocks
of this earth and phenomena in the sky at the same time".

John Keel, a later but similarly far-sighted American writer,
came to the conclusion that 'UFOs' were more likely to be "soft"

lightforms than "hard" metallic craft. As early as the 1960s, he was associating their appearance with areas ("windows") of geological faulting, earthquakes and geomagnetic anomaly. In France at about the same time, Ferdinand Lagarde was also noticing a significant correlation between reported 'UFOs' and geological faulting. Although there was no book dedicated solely to this approach within ufology at this time, American author Vincent H. Gaddis published *Mysterious Fires and Lights* (1967), which had chapters such as "Earth's Glowing Ghosts".

Historical literature has revealed that people from all cultures and times have seen unexplained light phenomena (Devereux 1982, 1989). To the Irish they were fairy lights, to the Scots they were simply *gealbhan* (balls of fire), to Malaysians, *pennangal* (the spectral heads of women who had died in childbirth), to Indians they were local deities or the lanterns of spirits, to Africans they were devil lights, to Brazilians the "Mother of Gold" leading to buried treasure, to Chinese Buddhists they were Bodhisattva Lights. (The Indians and Chinese sometimes built temples where lights appeared with some regularity.) Europeans visiting some of these lands also reported seeing strange lights – they were not just local lore. On a visit to Gabon in 1895, for instance, the writer Mary Kingsley saw a ball of violet light roll out of a wood onto the banks of Lake Ncovi; it hovered until joined by another, similar light. The two lightballs circled each other until Kingsley approached them in a canoe. One then flew off back into the trees while the other floated over the lake surface. As Kingsley paddled quickly after it, it went down into the water, still glowing as it sank. Locals later told her such phenomena were *aku*, devil lights.

In Europe there had been debate about unexplained lights from at least the medieval period. In the way that the popular myth today is that unidentified aerial phenomena (UAP) are extra-terrestrial craft, then it was that they were dragons. But some questioned this. In the 13th Century, for example, Albertus Magnus said the "dragons" were in actuality "vapours" that could roll into a ball and float up and down. In 1590, Thomas Hill said they were "fumes kindled" giving the simulacrum of a flying dragon. In 1608, Edward Topskell argued that "dragons" were really "a weaker kind of lightning".

There are also early modern reports from Britain, such as the account given in his *Journal* of 1830 by the "peasant poet", John Clare. He told how he encountered a lightball while walking one evening between the villages of Ashton and Helpston in Cambridgeshire. The light came towards him. "I thought it made a sudden stop as if to listen to me," he wrote. It crackled and was surrounded by a luminous halo: Clare described the light as having "a mysterious terrific hue". When it darted away Clare promptly took to his heels. He already knew that there was locally "a great upstir" about the lights, with up to fifteen at a time being seen over Deadmoor and Eastwell Moor flying back and forth, both with and against the wind. Clare said that his close encounter robbed him of "the little philosophical reasoning" he had about them.

In 1977, Michael Persinger and Gyslaine Lafrenière published *Space-Time Transients and Unusual Events*. Using a statistical approach, they correlated reported UFOs in North America with "seismic-related sources". They argued that the enormous energies built up in tectonic strain, *even without actual release in earthquakes*, were sufficient to produce glowing, ionised, lightforms in the atmosphere above such areas. Bodies of water, especially reservoirs, could also produce strain on underlying geology.

Over subsequent years, Persinger and the U.S. geologist John Derr, together and individually, examined specific "windows" of recurring reported light phenomena, and amassed an impressive

Figure 49. The late Michael Persinger

body of data to support this "tectonic strain theory". One such study was of the Yakima Indian reservation in Washington State, USA, where, in the 1970s, fire wardens in lookout posts observed and photographed a range of unusual light phenomena (along with weird ground-based poltergeist-type happenings). They saw large orange-coloured lightballs, smaller "ping-pong" balls of light, luminous columns and flares, and white lights with smaller, multi-coloured lights apparently connected to them. Glowing clouds and flashes in the sky were also noted. Derr and Persinger showed that three-quarters of the reported phenomena were seen most often in the vicinity of faulted ridges and they correlated outbreaks of the lights with seismic activity.

Another area where nature similarly lent researchers a hand is the Hessdalen valley near Trondheim, Norway. From late 1981, local people saw lights spring into visibility near rooftops, or hover just below the summits and ridges of the surrounding mountains. The lightforms included spheres and inverted "'bullet" and "Christmas tree" shapes. Colours were mainly white or yellow-white, though small, flashing red lights on the top or bottom of larger white forms were also reported. Strong, localised white or blue flashes in the sky were also observed. All rather similar to Yakima. In 1984, a group of researchers formed "Project Hessdalen" and conducted monitoring in Hessdalen using radar, magnetometers, spectrum analysers and other instrumentation. The group conducted further sessions in 1985 and 1986. Many photographs (some sequential) were taken of the lights, and radar anomalies were recorded. Around a decade later a new Project Hessdalen was inaugurated using more sophisticated automated monitoring equipment. Under the directorship of Erling Strand, it is still operating and real-time observation can be conducted from anyone's laptop by linking to their automatic station (www.hessdalen.org).

In 1980, Kevin and Sue McClure published *Stars and Rumours of Stars,* a thorough account of reported light phenomena in the

Figure 50. A Hessdalen light. [Photo: courtesy Project Hessdalen]

Figure 51. Llanfair chapel, south of Harlech in Wales. The field in the foreground lies on the Mochras Fault. In 1905, before the existence of the fault was known, multiple witnesses saw balls of red light emerge from the field and cavort in the air.

Barmouth-Harlech area of north-west coastal Wales in 1904-1905. Beriah Evans, a local journalist of the time, published accounts of witnesses' sightings, including his own: "Between us and the hills there suddenly flashed forth an enormous luminous star ... emitting from its whole circumference dazzling sparklets like flashing rays from a diamond ...". Glittering diamond-shapes were seen on roofs, "bottle-shaped" lights hung over hilltops, ruby-red lights popped out of the ground, rose into the air and fused together, and columns of light emerged from the ground.

London newsmen from the national daily papers who visited to report on the kerfuffle lost their initial cynicism when they saw the lights for themselves. The *Daily Mail* correspondent saw yellow balls of light of "electric vividness" hovering 100ft (30m) above the Barmouth-Harlech road. A *Daily Mirror* journalist found himself engulfed in a "soft, shimmering radiance".

Looking up, he saw "a large body" overhead that had "suddenly opened and emitted a flood of light from within itself".

As many of the reports contained location details, it seemed to me that this Welsh outbreak would be worth testing for geological links. So I teamed up with our Dragon Project geological adviser, Paul McCartney. It was our good fortune that a recent geological survey had been conducted in the area, enabling us to correlate exact sighting information with exact faulting information. It was found that there is the deep-rooted Mochras Fault almost linking Barmouth and Harlech, and that most of the lights events were strung out along it like scintillating beads on a thread.

Some sightings occurred off the main fault, but these were associated with tributary faulting. No reported light phenomenon occurred further than 700m (765 yards) from a fault, and incidence increased with proximity to faulting so that most events occurred within 100m (109 yards) of faulting. Indeed, some lights

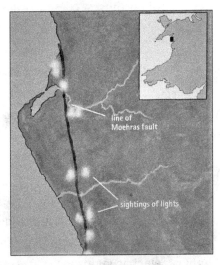

Figure 52. Sketch map of the Mochras Fault showing how incidents of light phenomena related to its course. (Other lights were also reported off the Mochras Fault, but they too related closely to secondary faulting.)

emerged directly out of the Mochras Fault. Further, it was found that the Welsh events began immediately after a local earthquake (in October, 1904).

Although this particular outbreak was an exceptional event in the area, the lights still appear occasionally. Harlech is adjacent to the Lleyn Peninsula, one of Britain's most active seismic zones. In 1984, it was the epicentre of a significant (5.5 Richter-scale) earthquake. A local resident told me that the evening before the quake he saw a brilliant white light "the size of a small car" float in from the sea and disappear into sand dunes.

In 1982, I published *Earth Lights* (with Paul McCartney). It was heavily attacked by UFO enthusiasts of an extra-terrestrial persuasion, and even by normally more reasonable research- ers who hadn't quite got their heads around this 'new' approach to anomalous aerial lights. In the same year, academic Helmut Tributsch published *When the Snakes Awake,* in which he recorded bizarre light phenomena (among other events) in association with earthquakes. The following year author Jenny Randles cited earth lights, or what she called unidentified aerial phenomena (UAP) sightings and made tectonic associations in her *The Pennine UFO Mystery.* In 1985, David Clarke and Granville Oldroyd published *Spooklights – A British Survey.* One of its well documented UAP haunts was at Burton Dassett, in south Warwickshire, the focus of outbreaks of light phenomena in 1922 and 1923. A reporter from the *Birmingham Post,* among other witnesses, saw a "steady and vivid" light travelling a few feet above the ground. Clarke and Oldroyd discovered that the location sits directly on the Burton Dassett fault, and that the mysterious light briefly reappeared on the night of 25 January, 1924. That very night, there was a power- ful earth tremor around Hereford, 60 miles (97km) to the west. This tectonic coincidence was noted by the local *Leamington*

Chronicle at the time. (This was a year after Fort had published his observations of apparent links between aerial lights and the 1896 Hereford-Worcester quake.) In 1989, I published *Earth Lights Revelation*. It included a section by David Clarke and Andy Roberts on Project Pennine, their study of the hill and moorland country running along the spine of England, an effort in which they were assisted by numerous other researchers. A geography of light-haunted moors, hills, valleys and reservoirs was mapped by the project, and phenomena described that ranged from balls of light to glowing hillsides. Clarke and Roberts expanded on this work in their *Phantoms of the Sky* (1990).

In the mid-1990s, under the aegis of the then Princeton-based International Consciousness Research Laboratories (ICRL), I was able to conduct some field expeditions with my wife Charla Devereux, another member of ICRL. We included a few of what in America are called "spook light" locations. These typically involve extremely long straight sections of road or former railroad corridors cutting through forests. The spook lights we investigated turned out to be distorted glimpses of distant vehicle headlights.

We paid two field visits to the famed 'Marfa lights' area of southern Texas, one along with the quantum physicist, Hal Puthoff. This turned out to be more complex. We conclusively showed that most of what people think are the Marfa lights seen from a designated viewing point are in fact distorted car headlights, 40 miles (64km) away, on the road going south to Presidio, or closer vehicles negotiating tracks leading to ranches out on the range, giving the appearance of lights dancing back and forth just above the slightly undulating ground. But there are reports of strange lights being seen in the vast region dating back to the 17th Century, and witnesses (including priests and teachers) we interviewed reported close encounters with spheres of lights. An 'active' area was seemingly the Chisos Mountains to the south of Marfa. There, I personally witnessed an anomalous light but it flickered out before photographs could be taken.

Finally, Erling Strand of Project Hessdalen and I investigated reported "min-min lights" in the remote Kimberley region of Australia. We gained insights from Indigenous Australians, and witnessed at least three probable UAP (one a beautiful, shimmering fan of golden light emerging soundlessly and momentarily from the desert surface). We managed to film only one of them, though – a moving white light that appeared as our magnetometer registered a strong geomagnetic reading – we identified this as relating to a powerful earthquake 800 miles away, so either that

Figure 53. Erling Strand, Director of Project Hessdalen, during one of many all-night observation sessions for 'min-min lights'/earth lights in remote outback Australia – a research fieldtrip conducted with the author. See text.

triggered the appearance of the light via geoelectrical changes, or it was a remarkable coincidence.

Some of these exploits, among others, were the subject of a 1996 Channel 4 documentary on British television (*Identified Flying Objects*, re-titled *Earth Lights* for Discovery Channel). It screened in November and marked an extraordinary coincidence that Fort would have hugely enjoyed: within twenty-four hours of transmission people began reporting bizarre light phenomena in Cornwall. There were soft, silent nocturnal luminous displays, rectangles of light moving jerkily through the heavens, and moon-like spheres that slowly dissolved. It went on all week, at the end of which Cornwall experienced its strongest earthquake of the century. (There's nothing like having Mother Earth as a PR agent!) These phenomena were later logged by a member of the British Geological Survey.

In 1997, Peter Brookesmith and I co-authored *UFOs and Ufology*, in which we tried to sort out all the strands that intertwined in the scene formerly known as 'ufology', including earth lights research and "alien abductions" (an altered state of consciousness issue, we decided, not an extra-terrestrial one). It was welcomed by genuine researchers but rubbished by diehard extra-terrestrial believers.

So, overall, the association of unusual light phenomena and geological faulting is fairly well established by various types of evidence spanning centuries. The lights were noted by past peoples and given explanations that were culturally relevant to their times. This, as we shall see in the Site Examples section below, did seemingly include the building of monuments where lights were seen.

While most reported sightings of strange aerial phenomena are surely the product of misperception of mundane objects, artificial or astronomical, or else mirage effects, hoaxes, or psycho-

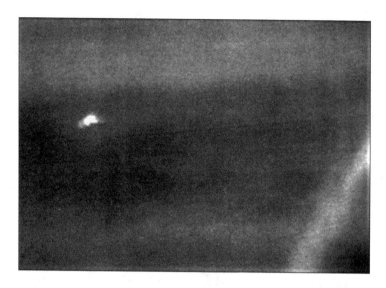

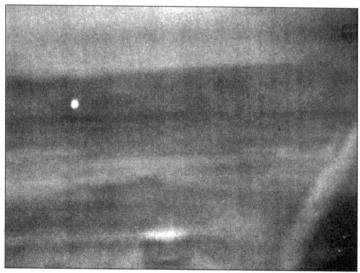

Figure 54. An apparent 'Min-Min'/earth light observed during our
Australian fieldtrip. *Top*: the light emerging. *Bottom*: the light clearing the
ground and moving away. This is remote, uninhabited outback landscape.
(The shape in the lower righthand corner of the frame is the edge of one
of our tents.) The magnetometer housed in another part of our field camp
simultaneously started registering an event – see text.

social factors affecting a witness's interpretation of a perception, there can be little doubt that there is a rump of reports that relates to genuinely unexplained luminous phenomena. It is at least a percentage of these core sightings that I think is comprised of earth lights, mystery lights, anomalous luminescences, or whatever we choose to call them.

These light phenomena seem to have electro-magnetic (EM) properties – Persinger suggested that they are surrounded by EM fields that can trigger hallucinations and trance states in close witnesses. Also, there are accounts of poltergeist-like events accompanying some outbreaks of light phenomena (such as at Yakima) with objects flying around, door latches moving of their own accord, and gravel crunching as if trod by ghostly feet. Interestingly, similar effects have been occasionally noted during particularly vivid aurorae events (Grant 1984 ibid.)

NATURE OF THE LIGHTS

The lights are presumably some exotic form of plasma. Plasmas can appear metallic in daylight – somewhat like air bubbles seen under water – and shine in the dark. But UAP can occasionally also appear totally black – perhaps an indication of a polarity-type effect. I well recall an incident in 1967, when I was a rear-seat passenger in a car one sunny summer afternoon somewhere around the Norfolk-Suffolk border in eastern England. I suddenly noticed a perfectly round, *perfectly* black shape just above treetop height over a roadside field. Another witness, in the passenger seat in front of me, also saw it. It maintained a horizontal course roughly parallel to the road, then vanished in front of our eyes. Moments later, the black shape reappeared a couple of fields away then shot upwards at an angle to be lost in the glare of the sun.

In talking to Erling Strand, I found he too had witnessed one of these pitch-black shapes, and Project Pennine also uncovered accounts of such phenomena. In addition, there are reports of black ball lightning in the literature (Tributsch 1982, ibid.).

Two other characteristics of earth lights are so bizarre that one hesitates to mention them. One is that according to witnesses far and wide, some lightballs seem to *react* to onlookers. John Keel, for instance, observed small lightballs in the Ohio Valley skittering about apparently to avoid his flashlight beam. Again, geologists in a jeep chasing after a Marfa light felt that it "definitely had intelligence". And several of the original Project Hessdalen people, including Erling Strand, have quietly admitted that in about ten percent of their observations they felt the lights interacted with them. If such reports have any credence, then some of these plasmas may possess rudimentary intelligence, often displayed as a playful, animal-like curiosity. But this is a forbidden topic. To even suggest that a form of consciousness might manifest in geophysical contexts as well as biological ones is to go beyond the pale. Nevertheless, laboratory studies in Romania have revealed cell-like forms within plasmas that can replicate, grow, and inter-communicate, and decades before the Romanian scientists made their observations, one of the fathers of plasma physics, David Bohm, was surprised to find that once electrons were in a plasma they stopped behaving like individuals and started behaving as if they were part of a larger and interconnected whole. He later remarked that he frequently had the impression that this sea of collective movements (Bohm diffusion) was *in some sense alive* (Keepin 1993).

The other highly exotic earth light/UAP characteristic sometimes reported might give the strongest clue to the deep nature of the phenomena. It revolves around quantum physics. If you have the technical means to examine any solid object closely enough, down through its constituent molecules and its atoms, it dissolves (as does all matter) into the weird sub-atomic quantum realm where peculiar properties prevail. Entanglement, for instance, in which electrons of an atom if separated can communicate with one another instantaneously over apparently any distance; or quantum events that are neither waves nor particles but *probabilities* that "collapse" into one or the other when subjected to attention. There are properties of earth lights that exhibit some of these quantum-like tendencies. As just one example, a *Daily Mirror* reporter who visited the Barmouth-Harlech lights outbreak recounted rushing towards a light shining like "an unusually brilliant carriage-lamp" barely 500 yards (457m) from him, but as he got closer it changed its form into a bar of intense blue light almost four feet (1m) long.

Figure 55. This anomalous light was photographed by trained physicist David Kubrin from the car park at Pinnacles National Monument, very close to the San Andreas Fault in California, in 1973. The light phenomenon flew at speed just above treetop height and displayed alternating effects of mass and weightlessness, in that it produced shockwaves in the air ahead of it while travelling, yet stopped dead without deceleration. It finally rotated rapidly and disappeared. The picture was taken just as this latter stage began. [Photo ©David Kubrin]

Observers on the other side of the light to the reporter could not see it at all even though there was nothing obscuring their view. Such unidirectional light emission has been reported in other anomalous light phenomena cases. This illogical, paradoxical effect, among others sometimes displayed by the lights, such as disappearing then reappearing instantaneously at another location or stopping seemingly without deceleration as if having no mass, makes me suspect that they are, somehow, *macro-quantal events.*

SITE EXAMPLES

Dyffryn Ardudwy Chambered Cairn, Wales.

This Neolithic megalithic site is in the village of Dyffryn Ardudwy, halfway between Harlech and Barmouth on the west coast of Wales. Originally, this monument was a single dolmen chamber inside a wedge-shaped cairn to which a second dolmen in its own round cairn was added shortly afterwards. Pottery fragments from near the first dolmen suggest a date of around 3000 B.C. for the site.

The monument sits directly on the Mochras Fault, and in 1904 and early 1905, as discussed above, there was an outbreak of well-documented light phenomena strung along it. This site was one of the hotspots for the phenomena. Here is an eyewitness account of an event that occurred in January 1905:

> The first form in which it appeared to me was that of a pillar of clear fire quite perpendicular. It was about two feet wide, and about three yards [9ft] in height. Suddenly another small fire began by its side some two yards distant ... and increased rapidly until it assumed the same size and form

Figure 56. Dyffryn Ardudwy dolmen, Wales. It sits directly adjacent to where strange lights were seen emerging from the ground. [Photo: Tanya Dedyukhina/Wikimedia Commons/CC BY 3.0]

... And as I gazed upon them I saw two arms of fire extending upwards from the top of each of the pillars ... I saw smoke ascending from the pillars, and immediately they began to disappear ... [and] became small and went out. It was a very wonderful fire. (McClure and McClure 1980)

Similar luminous columns were reported by other local inhabitants in the area. Balls and rods of light were also seen, mystery glows on the mountains, and all the other forms associated with earth light phenomena.

The remains of other important megalithic monuments dot the area, following the local fault lines.

Delphi, Greece

Even legend identifies this place with faulting, as according to which the site of this major oracle temple on the lower slopes of Mount Parnassus was discovered accidentally by a herds-man, Koretas, who happened across a chasm or fissure at the spot. Fumes issuing from it put him into a trance in which he saw visions of the future. A timber oracle house dedicated to the Earth Goddess, Gaia, was built there. A further legend states that when the young god, Apollo, later came across the place, by then called Pytho, he encountered and killed the she-dragon, the python, that dwelt there. The Pythian Games were instituted to commemorate this mythic event, which in actuality seems to be a mythic encoding of the usurpation of a Bronze Age goddess shrine by a later Apollo cult.

The oracle of Delphi was active for over a thousand years, and kings, generals and regular folk came from far and wide to consult it. The prophetess, or *Pythia* (there were many over the years), issued the oracular pronouncements in the Temple of Apollo, and its ruins standing there today, dating from the 4th Century B.C., are on the site of the earlier stone and timber

Figure 57. The ruined Temple of Apollo, Delphi, Greece.

shrines. The Prophetess would purify herself before an oracular session by bathing in and drinking from the nearby Castalian spring at the foot of the mountain, and would also drink the waters from the Kassotis spring that ran into the temple itself. It is said that the Pythia would then burn laurel leaves with barley on an altar before entering the oracle chamber, the *Mantion*, where she was attended by priests. No other woman was allowed there. The client would go into a room adjoining the oracle chamber and write his question on a lead tablet. The Pythia seated herself on a tripod – a tall, three-legged stool with a bowl-like seat – and held a laurel leaf in one hand she occasionally shook. She would go into trance and utter the oracular response to the question asked, usually in a kind of verse.

The true nature of the actual prophetic session at Delphi has long remained a vexed question among scholars. Did the Pythia really go into a prophetic trance or was it simply an act

Figure 58. An image on a drinking cup (kylix) from Vulci (c.430 B.C.), showing King Aigeus consulting the Pythia at Delphi, seated on her tripod.

for the gullible? There have been protagonists for both views. Some of those arguing for a genuine trance point to the tradition of the burning of laurel leaves by the Pythia. It had been supposed by some that this smoke might have been psychoactive, but Albert Hofmann, the Swiss chemist who synthesised LSD, was unable to find any chemically active principles in laurel that could induce altered mind states. This was supported in self-experimentation by the Princeton psychologist, Julian James: he crushed laurel leaves and smoked quantities of them in a pipe. He felt somewhat sick, "but no more inspired than usual" (Jaynes 1976).

Prime candidate for a trance-inducing agent at Delphi, however, has been the belief that the temple of Apollo was situated over the fuming fissure discovered by Koretas, and that the tripod was designed to suspend the prophetess over it in order that she would be able to inhale the fumes and thus enter into the prophetic trance. Classical scholars have long rejected this idea, considering that the whole concept of the toxic vapour was simply romantic myth. This scepticism, though, has subsequently been challenged by geologist Jelle de Boer and colleagues (de Boer 2001). He has claimed to have identified an active geological fault to the east and west of the temple of Apollo, presumably passing beneath the temple. The faulting was exposed by roadworks, which de Boer feels explains why early researchers had not detected it. He also found another, smaller, fault running approximately north-south, connecting with the main fault at the temple. This faulting has created cracks in the rocks that could open and close during periods of seismic activity. In the rock strata below Delphi is a limestone layer rich in hydrocarbons, and because Delphi is in an active quake zone it is feasible that gases such as ethylene, methane and hydrogen sulphide could be sporadically released during tectonic stress and strain, and vented out through the rock fissures into the open air. De Boer suggests that such gases could have intoxicated the Pythia. (If these observations are true, then the Delphi prophetesses were, in effect, the ancient forerunners of today's glue sniffers!) The old legend of Koretas may therefore contain more than a whiff of truth. There remains some debate about this research, but the basics of the researchers' findings remain. Delphi may have been usurped by Apollo, but the place most definitely belongs to Gaia.

The Kos Asclepeion

Asclepeions were scattered across the whole sphere of influence of Ancient Greece. On the Greek island of Kos in the Aegean, is an Asclepeion that could be reasonably argued to be the birthplace of modern medicine. The island is where the father of modern medicine, Hippocrates, was born (c.460 B.C.). He was a real person and, unlike Asclepius, not a mythical god. There was already a circle of physicians on Kos, and his father and grandfather were Asclepiades – physician-priests in the cult of Asclepius. He ultimately came to teach medicine outside the self-acclaimed "family circle" of Asclepiades. Nevertheless, he was born into the medical environment of his time and made great use of it, learning all there was to know from some of the best contemporary teachers available and, importantly, coming to analyse and classify the wide range of diseases suffered by the people coming to various Asclepeions – he travelled to mainland Greece, especially to Thessaly, to Egypt and elsewhere. Eventually, he was to lay down new, objective guidelines for medicine, removing it from the spheres of religion and superstition. He included environmental, dietary and lifestyle factors in treatment. He also placed much importance on the ethics and professional discipline of physicians – the Hippocratic Oath, is, of course, acknowledged to this day. He established his school of medicine on Kos and the Kos Asclepeion, built after Hippocrates' death, adopted some of its principles.

The Asclepeion is located in the foothills of Mount Dikaios, where a sacred grove to Apollo formerly existed, and is built in three tiers or terraces that seat it harmoniously into the landscape. The site was considered to offer a perfect balance of air, land and water. The temple was active and important throughout much of the Hellenistic era (323 – 146 B.C.), and features within its precinct today derive from different time periods. Much of the original Asclepeion has disappeared due to earthquakes, testifying to its seismic location, and the use of it as a handy source of stones by the Knights of St. John, but an overall impression of the place can still be obtained. Until relatively recently it was fed by springs on the mountain providing waters containing iron, sulphur, calcium, and carbonic acid. Not only was water important from a purification point of view, hydrotherapy was a key part of the Asclepeion's range of treatments and was particularly focused on the first, lower, terrace where it is believed the school of medicine was situated.

Castlerigg Stone Circle, Cumbria, England.

Situated about a mile east of the town of Keswick in the Lake District of England, the siting of this magnificent stone circle is amongst the most impressive in Britain, commanding a surrounding skyline view of rugged Lakeland hills. The site itself is well preserved, with its stones forming a flattened circle 33.5m

Figure 59. The Castlerigg stone circle, Cumbria.

(110ft) across its longest diameter. Inside the main ring of stones is a mysterious rectangular setting of up to ten stones, often referred to as 'The Cove'. A gap flanked by two large stones in the northern arc of the circle was probably an original entrance. In all, there are thirty-eight surviving stones at the site, the heaviest weighing around fifteen tons.

During a 1988 visit by the Dragon Project, all the Castlerigg stones were checked for any magnetic anomalies with liquid-filled compasses. Only one of the thirty-eight stones affected the compass needle: the leaning westernmost stone. It's inwards-facing side strongly deflects a compass needle in one area, and attracts it in another.

But the main reported 'energy' interest relating to this site occurred in the early years of the 20th Century. Writing in *English Mechanic and the World of Science* in 1919, a Mr T. Sington described an experience he and an acquaintance had around Easter time some years earlier. The two men were returning to their hotel in Keswick in darkness, after an ascent of Helvellyn. Here is Sington's account:

When we were at a point near which the track branches
off to the Druidical circle [Castlerigg], we all at once saw
a rapidly moving light ... and we instinctively stepped to
the road boundary wall to make way for it, but nothing
came ... It was a white light, and having crossed the road
it disappeared...

We then saw a number of lights possibly a third of a mile or
more away, directly in the direction of the Druidical circle,
but, of course, much fainter, no doubt due to distance,
moving backwards and forwards horizontally; we stood
watching them for a long time ... Whilst we were watching,
a remarkable incident happened – one of the lights, and only
one, came straight to the spot where we were standing; at
first very faint, as it approached the light increased in intensity ... But when it came close to the wall it slowed down,
stopped, quivered, and slowly went out, as if the matter
producing the light had suddenly become exhausted. It was
globular, white with a nucleus possibly 6 feet [2m] or so in
diameter, and just high enough above ground to pass over
our heads...

The lights we saw all moved horizontally, never vertically, or
at an angle; they moved in opposite directions at the same
time, therefore they were not affected by any air currents.

Sington concluded his account by wondering why the site of the
stone circle had been selected. "Suppose, owing to some local
condition at present unknown," he mused, "such lights have
occurred from time to time near the site, they would have attract-
ed the attention of the inhabitants, who, awestruck, would have

attached great significance to them, and might then have selected the site as a place of worship or sacrifice."

So, for his time, Sington's thinking was remarkably perceptive.

Sacred Lights

We know for sure that certain ancient temple sites in Asia were built to honour light phenomena. Two examples in one place, for instance – two pilgrimage shrines dedicated to the Goddess Bhagbatti on the sacred Purnagiri Mountain of northern India were built because of local light phenomena. The lights are said to be votive lamps lit by a holy man in worship of the goddess. In his *The Temple Tiger* (1934, and many later editions), Jim Cobbett describes his visit to the temples, which can only be accessed by a narrow cliff-path, in which he witnessed three strange lights, each about two feet (60cm) in diameter, in a gorge. One light merged slowly with another, then more lights appeared. They glowed in front of a sheer rock face. Or, again, the sacred Chinese mountains of Wu Tai Shan and Omei Shan apparently have, or at least had, large golden-orange lightballs frequent their peaks at night. These were interpreted as 'Bodhisattva Lights'. In his book, *The Wheel of Life* (1959), traveller and adventurer John Blofeld described a visit in 1937 to Wu T'ai, where he found there was a tower on a temple constructed specifically to view the Bodhisattva Lights. The windows of the tower "overlooked miles and miles of empty space", Blofeld remarked. He and a group of companions were staying overnight at the temple, and just after midnight a monk rushed into their room and roused them, saying the Bodhisattva had appeared. Although it was bitterly cold, Blofeld and his friends climbed up into the tower. From it they saw "innumerable balls of fire" floating by, though because of the vast void of space in which they were suspended it proved impossible to judge their distance and therefore their size. "Fluffy balls of orange-coloured fire, moving through space, unhurried and majestic – truly a fitting manifestation of divinity!" Blofeld exclaimed.

Oracular Caves

Natural places were also selected for the same sort of geological-based reasons that gave rise to the founding of Delphi – they issued mind-altering fumes. In the greater eastern Mediterranean region such selected natural places were usually caves. These were typically seen in ancient Greece as entrances to the underworld, to Hades, and were often referred to as 'Plutonia' or 'Charonia', referring, respectively, to Pluto, lord of the underworld, and Charon, the ferryman of souls across the River Styx. These were used as oracles of the dead, *nekuomanteia*, including a famous one at Avernus near Cumae in southern Italy.

In the Meander Valley in Asia Minor (largely, today's Turkey) there were three celebrated Charonia – at Hierapolis, at Acharaca, and the Aornum near Magnesia. These oracles were located in an area where 'noxious vapours' rose from the ground. These gases could be dangerous and deadly as well as mind-altering:

> For instance, at Hierapolis (modern Pamukkale) there was a deep cave with a narrow opening filled with misty poisonous vapours, which killed every animal entering the cave. Only the eunuch priests of the goddess Cybele were able to enter the cave, either due to their techniques of holding their breath, or antidotes … The Plutonium has been identified: it is a deep chamber and a hole, emitting highly poisonous gases. Thus, ancient accounts of gas discharge have been verified by modern scientists and found [to be] precise. (Ustinova 2009)

There were numerous other such gas-emitting caves designated as oracles in the general region.

Airigh na Beinne Bige, Callanish (Calanais), Isle of Lewis, Scotland

This site, also known more prosaically as Site X1, now consists of a single standing stone on an open hillside overlooking the main Callanish Stones site less than 3km away. A survey using remote geophysical sensing techniques has revealed that the standing stone was actually part of what had been a stone circle at the site. But the survey revealed something even more startling – the former ring of stones had encircled a powerful magnetic anomaly about 20m across marked by a star-like feature interpreted by the investigating archaeologists as resulting from an ancient and massive single lightning strike, or multiple strikes. The deeply engraved marking lies on the rock surface beneath the present-

Figure 60. The geophysically acquired image of the star-like marking on the rock surface beneath Site X1, Callanish, Isle of Lewis, Scotland. The former ring of stones are lightly marked in this picture. [Courtesy of Dr. C. Richard Bates]

day peat bog covering and so dates to at least 3,000 years old. As Professor Vincent Gaffney, one of the five investigating researchers, has remarked: "This was completely and utterly unexpected. Seeing the evidence for a massive strike, right in the middle of what now seems to be a stone circle, is remarkable."

The finding is part of a project by researchers from three universities exploring the use of various geophysical survey methods to study ancient landscapes. (Bates et al. 2019)

Obviously, the speculation arises as to whether the lightning event(s) inspired the building of the Neolithic stone circle at that specific spot. It seems to have been an incredible coincidence if that wasn't the case. Various commentators have wondered if it was actually just a lightning strike: could the star-like feature have been created by the impact of ball lightning (or its close cousin, an earth light)? Various possible factors spring to mind. One is that the Callanish main circle and its satellite sites cluster closely around a pattern of local faulting, as we have already seen. Another, whether relevant or not, is that the Dragon Project measured radiation levels at the Callanish sites and found them to be up to thirty times the average regional background levels (Devereux 1990). A third and important factor is that a strange light, which accrued folklore around it, was seen fairly regularly "for generations" within a few miles of Callanish (Magin 1987). In fact, reports of earth light phenomena have been made for untold numbers of years on the island.

* * * * *

So, temples were built in in China and India that were seemingly dedicated to the observation of earth lights, which were identified within the contexts of their various cultures as being gods or bodhisattvas. It thus is no stretch to consider that the Neolithic megalith builders could have reacted to strange lights in a similar way, within the frames of their own beliefs and understanding. We might usefully remind ourselves of T. Sington's comments with regard to light phenomena at the Castlerigg stone circle:

> Suppose, owing to some local condition at present unknown, such lights have occurred from time to time near the site, they would have attracted the attention of the inhabitants, who, awestruck ... might then have selected the site as a place of worship or sacrifice.

4

SOUND

It is easy to overlook the fact that sound is a physical force, and too easy to forget that ancient, prehistoric people had ears: when we visit an ancient site we so often tend to imagine what we think went on there as if in a kind of silent movie. In fact, sonic energy, sound, is particularly germane to archaeological study – it is certainly a power some ancient sacred places possess – yet it is only in the last couple of decades that the potential acoustical dimension has really begun to be considered and investigated in a serious way. It is now called 'archaeoacoustics'. And it is only recently, in fact, that this aspect has been added to part of the Dragon Project's current brief.

There are various ways in which ancient places can 'speak'.

VOICES OF THE ROCKS

Petroglyph Rock (aka "The Teaching Rocks") in Peterborough Provincial Park, Ontario, is a large, sloping marble slab covered with several hundred ancient engravings – it is said to be the most carved rock in the whole of Canada. Other exposed rock surfaces around are devoid of such carvings, so why was that particular rock sought out as such a special place a thousand or more years ago?

The answer most probably lies with a fissure about 16 feet (5m) deep that cuts across the rock's surface. Ground water

Figure 61. Petroglyph Rock ("The Teaching Rocks"), Peterborough
Provincial Park, Ontario. (Courtesy © Ontario parks)

sporadically flows along the bottom of the fissure causing noises
remarkably like whispering voices to issue forth. American
Indians (First Nation people) in this part, like many other parts,
of the Americas had a belief that spirits, *manitous*, lived inside
certain rocks and behind cliff-faces (Rajnovich 1994), so voice-
like sounds emerging from this rock would readily have been
identified as the spirits speaking. It is easy to understand, therefore, why it became a sacred place, perhaps even an oracle centre,
thus accounting for the profusion of rock carvings on its surface.

Rocks that could produce animal-like sounds probably
had especially magical properties for hunters. One that fits this
description is the Blowing Stone, to be found in southern England
at the village of Kingston Lisle, in the Vale of the White Horse
in Oxfordshire. The rock is now no longer in precisely its original location, which was local, but is in an area rich in prehistoric
monuments, including the Uffington White Horse hill figure. The
Blowing Stone is a natural cube-like block of rock about 3 feet

(1m) tall, pierced by several holes due to natural weathering or to vegetation growing into it over centuries when it lay in the ground. One of these holes is the opening to a Y-shaped channel in the rock, and when blown into by someone proficient in playing wind instruments produces a sound alleged to be audible up to six miles (10km) distant. It was described in Thomas Hughes' *Tom Brown's Schooldays* as being a "gruesome sound somewhere between a moan and a roar, sounding over the valley ... a ghost-like awful voice". In fact, the sound is closely reminiscent of the bellow of a stag or elk, and so may have been used in hunting rituals, or even to attract quarry in the surrounding landscape.

Figure 62. The Blowing Stone, Kingston Lisle, Oxfordshire – making it 'speak'.

ECHOES AND SPIRITS

Echoes would have reinforced the ancient belief in rock-dwelling spirits, and would probably have influenced the choice for locating many ancient rock art sites around the world. First Nation people in Canada, for instance, considered places (often marked by swatches of red ochre paint) where cliffs rise directly out of water to be favoured haunts of the rock *manitous*, which is interesting because such locations are also particularly effective in the propagation of echoes – the water surface acts as a kind of amplifier and transmitter.

Algonquin shamans in trance believed that they could pass in spirit through rock surfaces to obtain "rock medicine" or supernatural power from "the men-within-the-rocks". This belief of a spirit world inside rocks or cliffs was held by many American Indian peoples – certain rock art in California, for example, shows human figures exiting or entering cracks in rock surfaces (Whitley 1996). Indeed, other peoples around the world held similar beliefs – it is known to have existed with the Bushmen (San) in southern Africa (Dowson 1992; Dowson & Lewis-Williams 1989), for instance, and the anthropologist, Paul Wirtz, noted that the indigenous people of New Guinea acknowledged special rocks they called 'soimi' stones:

> From each *soimi* stone there emanate certain powerful influences which correspond with those of the spirit-being (*uaropo*) intimately dwelling within it. These forces, whether for the benefit of individuals or the community as a whole, the people seek to turn to profit and advantage. (Wirtz cited in Levy-Bruhl 1935)

As we shall see, the Chinese considered that rocks were condensed forms of that mysterious universal energy, *ch'i*. We moderns take sound for granted in our noisy world, but to ancient peoples who did not have our scientific model for sound, it could be mysterious, magical.

Someone who has spent many years studying echoes and rock art is American researcher, Steven Waller. Waller had noted passing phrases in the rock art literature to the "acoustic space" in caverns, and that echoes at rock art sites were "a phenomenal attribute" of them. He had also read papers by French-based researcher Iegor Reznikoff (1995), who had been exploring Palaeolithic painted caves with the human voice, checking relationships between echoes and the rock art in those places. But it was a personal experience in 1987 that really fired Waller's interests. He was standing outside the mouth of a prehistoric painted cave in France when he became struck by the psychological power of echoes "'mysteriously' emanating from the cave in answer to sounds made outside" (Waller 1993). He realised that in the period preceding the modern scientific understanding of acoustics, echoes and reverberation phenomena would have been thought of as being spontaneously generated noises that would have bestowed a magical aura to such locations as caves and canyons that reflect sound.

Waller carried out some experiments by making different kinds of noises in a variety of acoustic environments. He discovered that when rocks are struck together in the manner of making stone tools, echoes sound remarkably like the feet of galloping horses. He learned that a majority of the animal figures depicted in Palaeolithic rock art were animals as well as creatures such as mammoths with hard pounding feet, so he decided to test the acoustic responses to percussive effects in places where such rock art existed. The method employed by Waller involved the making of a given set of single, loud, percussive sounds – striking rocks, clapping hands, yelling in sharp vocal bursts and using a spring-loaded device capable of making a percussive sound of reproducible intensity at a level comparable to natural clapping. After the generation of each single percussive sound, the direction was noted from which the resulting reflected sound was heard, and it was subjectively judged for its characteristics. In addition, acoustic equipment was deployed for quantitative testing – a high-quality tape recorder and microphone, and precision sound-level meters. During the on-site recordings the same positioning of the recording equipment relative to the original sound source was maintained at all the locations. Playback of the recordings was by means of an auditorium sound system, through which the primary percussive burst, the subsequent reflected sound and the background ambient noise at each site were isolated and measured separately.

Waller sampled a selection of rock art sites in France. As a general pattern, he found the echoes vibrate at an average level of 3 decibels (dB) in the caves, but rock art panels of hoofed animals produced reflected sound of 23-31 dB. Panels showing feline creatures, on the other hand, averaged a much lower 1-7 dB. Unpainted rock surfaces tended to be totally acoustically flat.

Waller has continued to study many such sites acoustically, and gone on much further afield than France. He encountered some remarkable acoustic effects in Australia, for instance, where ancient Aboriginal rock art is typically painted on the curved walls of rock shelters. When he placed himself about 100 feet (30m) from an Aboriginal painted wall, echoes seem to emanate from the central images, but when he made noise closer into the wall, it reflected back too quickly to be distinguished

Figure 63. Ancient Aboriginal rock painting on the curved wall of a rock shelter.

from the original sound. "It was almost spooky," Waller admitted. This type of acoustic phenomenon is due to the curved rock walls acting in a similar way to a parabolic mirror focusing light.

Tommaso Mattioli and colleagues have been studying echoes and rock art sites using somewhat sophisticated methods, conducting research in the rock art landscapes of Baume Brune (Vaucluse, France) and Valle d'Ividoro (Puglia, Italy). In these two echoing areas only a few rock shelters were chosen to be painted with rock art in preference to other, undecorated shelters. Why should this be? "Modern studies in psychoacoustics demonstrate that some people have the capacity to locate places and orientate themselves by identifying the exact location where echoes and sound reflections came from. This ability, usually observed in blind people - but also in sighted people that have been trained – is called echolocation. Was echolocation used in the past?" they wondered.

They conducted fieldwork using a sound generator, sound recorder, and spherical camera, and measured the impulse response. "The processed results indicate that there was a positive relationship between sound-reflecting surfaces and the location of rock art," they reported. "This leads us to propose that in both areas [under study] there is a strong probability of echolocation having been employed by Neolithic people to select the shelters in which to produce rock art. The results obtained in our study also have wider implications in our understanding of how prehistoric peoples perceived the landscape in which they lived, understood not only on the basis of tangible elements but, perhaps more importantly, because of intangible aspects such as sound and, in particular, echoes." (Mattioli T. et al. 2017)

Even today, and probably reaching back into antiquity, there are traditional echo technicians – such as the throat-singers in Tuvan, an autonomous republic within the Russian Federation. They developed their vocal art originally as a means of interacting sonically with their natural environment, not for entertainment. Throat-singing involves the production of resonant sounds, overtones and whistles within the throat, nasal cavities, mouth and lips, and was used to provoke echoes or imitate natural sounds like waterfalls or wind. The master throat singers can still select precise locations inside caves where the resonances are exactly right to maximise the reverberations of their songs. They even wait until the atmospheric conditions are perfect for the greatest effect. It is in essence a technology of echoes. At one locale, where a singer called Kaigal-ool performed in front of a cliff-face, ethnomusicologist Theodore Levin reported that "the cliff and surrounding features sing back to the musician in what Kaigal-ool calls 'a kind of meditation – a conversation that I have with nature'" (Levin 2006).

STONE AGE BROADCASTING AND RECEPTION

Apart from the general matter of echoes, there are a variety of other forms of environmental acoustic phenomena that can manifest at or around a sacred site. One is the manner in which sound can behave in unusual ways in the open at certain places. Consider, for instance, Writing Rock, a white granite boulder in the Cheyenne River Valley in North Dakota. This is indented with cupules and incised with markings and is located close to a spring with panoramic views – a typical vision-quest location. It is also set within a natural amphitheatre with such exceptional acoustics that people talking across the valley and in other distant locations are perfectly audible; by the same token it has been suggested that the sound of the rock being pounded would have transmitted long distances through the valley. In similar vein, the Herschel petroglyph site in Saskatchewan, Canada, has been noted as being a resonant location where sounds can be amplified. The site had been used by Indians as a buffalo jump where herds of bison were stampeded over a precipice to be killed and butchered below. It has been suggested that the special acoustic qualities of the place would have amplified the sounds produced in the making of hundreds of cupules hammered into a monolithic rock there mimicking the sound of a bison herd on the move.

Specific types of site can also transmit or receive sound on an environmental scale. A version of this particular effect occurs at the White Shaman rock shelter. This site is situated on a canyon side in the Lower Pecos region of Texas, close by the border with Mexico, at the confluence of the Pecos River and the Rio Grande. It is one of numerous painted rock shelters in the canyons of the two merging rivers and was discovered in 1952 by Jim Zintgraff and a companion.

Figure 64. General view of the White Shaman Shelter showing some of the rock wall paintings. (The White Shaman image is at left in this picture.)

The shelter contains remarkable multi-coloured panels painted on its curved rock wall. They are largely in what is termed 'Pecos River style', dated to c. 2100-1200 B.C. The imagery contains over thirty anthropomorphic figures, many in the characteristic form of long rectangular bodies, short legs, stubby outstretched arms and small rectangular heads as well as no heads at all. Some have a black band running down the centre of the body and these are referred to as 'centrastyled' figures and are often considered to be depictions of shamans. In addition, there are animal figures and geometric imagery, including over a hundred dots, some free-floating with others associated with specific images. The shelter gained its name from a panel showing a white centrastyle depiction of a human figure apparently floating up out of another very similar-shaped but dark anthropomorphic form. It might be the earliest prehistoric depiction of the so-called out-of-body experience, probably induced by the ritual use of psychoactive drugs.

Figure 65. Detail of the 'White Shaman'. The white figure is roughly
1.5m (5ft) tall.

This is a strong likelihood. Archaeologist and artist Caroline Boyd has made the connection between Lower Pecos rock art and the imagery found in textiles produced by the regionally close Huichol Indians in Mexico (Boyd 1998). This textile imagery is based on visions induced in ritual ingestion of the hallucinogenic cactus, peyote, and direct evidence has been found of prehistoric usage of peyote (and other mind-altering plant substances) in the rock shelters of the Lower Pecos.

Notwithstanding the dramatic painted panels in the shelter, Zintgraff recalls that the acoustics of the place caught his attention at the time of discovery (Zintgraff 2005, personal communication.). In terms of echoes, I confirmed during a visit to the site that a loud voice directed specifically at the White Shaman panel produces exceptional echoes from the other side of the canyon, approximately 150m distant. Entire words can echo back and it is possible to hear fainter, secondary and tertiary echoes from farther down the canyon. It requires only a minimum effort of the imagination to gain the impression of the canyon as being full of spirits – one can only guess how the echoes would have affected someone in a profoundly altered state of consciousness in a given cultural context.

Also, conversation conducted in a normal talking pitch within the rock shelter transmits with perfect fidelity to points on the opposite side of the canyon, well beyond normal earshot (Zintgraff 2005, Boyd 2005 personal comments). Further, in one experiment, five drums were beaten within the rock shelter by American Indian drummers and the sound produced was broadcast so effectively that traffic stopped on a highway over a kilometre distant – apparently, drivers got out of their vehicles to investigate the source of the sound. Another discovery at this remarkable acoustic site concerns unusually deep mortar holes in the floor of the rock shelter – they can act in drum-like fashion when pestles are thrust down into them, causing the whole site to broadcast resonant sounds (Boyd 2005, personal communication).

At least two rock art sites in southern California have similarly been found to variously receive or transmit sound on a landscape scale (Hedges 1993). One of these, Wikwip (Echo Rock), in San Diego County, is a rock shelter in a distinctive rock formation visible from a distance; a characteristic of the rock shelter, which is known to have been a ceremonial site of Kumeyaay Indians, is that it focuses sound within itself so that conversation can be heard in it from 100m outside. Another rock shelter in the same county, at Canebrake Wash, does the reverse – conversation in front of the paintings in it is broadcast into the surrounding landscape.

Tommaso Mattioli and Margarita Diaz-Andreu have followed up on this line of investigation with an innovative approach in the Sierra de San Serván area in Extremadura, Spain (Mattioli and Diaz-Andreu 2017). There are hundreds of rock shelters in this area but only sixty-five contain prehistoric rock imagery. Using sophisticated electronic field equipment to systematically 'listen' to the landscape in the open and in the rock shelters, they collected raw acoustic data which was analysed by a method called 'Transmission Loss' to determine the audibility of distant sounds. Their results showed that the decorated rock shelters picked up distant sounds much more effectively than non-decorated ones. The decorated rock shelters could be likened to 'rock ears', able to discern distant sounds further away and more intelligibly compared to the 'deafness' of the shelters without rock art. In other words, the shape of the decorated rock shelters markedly augmented the sounds coming into them from the outside world. The prehistoric people making the rock art clearly deliberately chose such shelters; the reason cannot be known for sure, but it is fairly obvious that these places by sensitively receiving the sounds

Figure 66. Aaron Watson (right) and David Keating testing the acoustics at Stonehenge.

in the environment would offer greater safety by speedily warning of any approaching, unseen dangers, and also would aid in the location and hunting of animals.

Sound behaviour within constructed monumental sites has also started to be mapped. Aaron Watson and David Keating, then of Reading University, deployed an amplifier and a digital audio-recorder with omni-directional microphone at a range of megalithic sites. The amplifier issued pink noise – that is, sound with a wide frequency spectrum. They observed the behaviour of the sound at a variety of recumbent stone circles in Scotland, such as Easter Aquorthies (mentioned earlier in a different context, and see Figure 23) and found the recumbent stone to act like a stage, so an officiant singing, uttering or playing music in front of it would project sounds into the centre of the circle, with returning echoes from the perimeter standing stones, which increase in size and thus reflective effectiveness towards the recumbent block. The distribution of stronger sound was contained almost exclusively within the circumference of the stone circle. In a sense, the Reading pair conjured the ghosts of Stone Age ritualists standing at specific spots in the stone circles they investigated (Watson and Keating 1999, 2000).

Inevitably, they had to acoustically test Stonehenge. They were able to map how the passage of sound was augmented or attenuated among the giant stones, and they noted evidence that the faces of some of the inner faces of the sarsen uprights had been shaped by stone mauls into concave surfaces that reflected and directed sounds within the interior of the monument.

In Orkney, at the massive stone block of the Dwarfie Stane, which has chambers and passages that were hewn out of the solid rock in Neolithic times, these researchers encountered another odd phenomenon: when they set up a resonant frequency inside the chamber using their voices, they found that the massive stone block and the air within it appeared to shake vigorously. The vibration was also evident to people standing outside on top of the tomb. So the *sensation* of moving stone blocks could be achieved by the use of sound. (Watson and Keating 2000 ibid.)

RESONANCE

Acoustical resonance is another way sonic energy can occur at a prehistoric monument – but they have to be chambered monuments. In the mid-1990s, a small team from the then Princeton University based International Consciousness Research Laboratories (ICRL – www.icrl.org) led by the late Professor Robert Jahn, acoustically tested a small, random selection of chambered megalithic sites in southern England and Ireland for their primary resonant frequencies – that is, the lowest frequency at which a standing acoustical wave occurs. To put that more technically, when sound waves of equal amplitude meet each other in 'constructive interference' – i.e. when the waves' "crests" (antinodes) and "troughs" (nodes) reinforce one another. When a sound source within a Neolithic chamber is tuned through the lower audible range until a sound wave of equal amplitude is reflected off the walls (thus producing a standing wave) then the lowest natural resonance of the chamber cavity has been attained.

The ICRL investigators used an omni-directional loudspeaker as a sound source driven by a variable frequency sine-wave oscillator, and a 20-watt amplifier. This was linked to a digital multimeter to verify frequencies. The frequencies coming from the sound source were manually swept until the lowest natural resonance of the chamber became clearly discernible. The loudness was then adjusted to the highest comfortable level, and a

Figure 67. The ICRL equipment used during its mid-1990s
investigations into the resonance of Neolithic chambers.

measured grid or measuring tape was laid on the ground enabling
radial horizontal mapping of the acoustic standing waves within
the chamber to be made with sound-level meters.

To the surprise of the researchers all the investigated
chambers were found to resonate in a 95-120 Hz frequency band,
with most at 110-112 Hz, and particularly focused on 110 Hz. This
was despite variations in sizes and shapes of the chambers, and
there was even some evidence of 'retro-fitting', as if features like
standing stones and recesses in walls within the chambers had
been deliberately placed to help 'tune' the resonant frequency
(Jahn et al. 1996).

This frequency range is at the lower baritone level, and the
simplest interpretation is that adult male voices were used in these
supposed tombs for the silent dead. This could have been in the
form of chanting or for oracular purposes, in either case probably conducted at those times of year marked by the entrance of
sunbeams into the chambers (most of the selected monuments

are astronomically oriented). But was there anything special about this acoustical frequency? It wouldn't seem so on the face of it, but a colleague in the ICRL group, neuroclinician Ian Cook of UCLA's Neuropsychiatric Institute, was asked if he would check for any effects of the 110 Hz audio frequency on the human brain. So, Cook and colleagues took a group of thirty healthy individuals who were asked to listen to pure tones at each of five frequencies (90, 100, 110, 120, and 130 Hz) as they rested with eyes closed. The duration of each tone was approximately one minute and was presented through speakers positioned near the subjects' ears. Quantitative EEG (QEEG) recordings were made to measure activity in the subject's brains during the process. The results showed that at 110 Hz activity in the frontal cortex was virtually reversed right lobe-left lobe from the averaged trend that was being monitored in the subjects during the other frequencies. It was almost as if a switch had been thrown. (There were also other brain changes in the temporal cortex at that frequency we needn't go into here.) (Cook 2003; Cook et al. 2008)

The full implications of this finding require further investigation, and what it might mean for an individual's mind state, but there has been scant such work since. However, later acoustic investigation of El Castillo cave system in Monte Castillo near Puente Viesgo, Spain, has yielded intriguing supportive information. Evidence of human use of the cave dates back over 40,000 years. A strange, carved stalagmite located within what appears to have been a ritual chamber and presumed focus of shamanic practices within the cave system was singled out for study.

A range of audio tones (80Hz – 1kHz) were generated at the location. The sound was simultaneously recorded within the same cave at a position where an audience would observe the ritual. Subsequent analyses identified a frequency-dependent amplification of recorded sound intensity for frequencies approaching 100 Hz, with the greatest effect observed at 108 and 110 Hz. In a concluding technical discussion, the researchers state:

> Quantitative support of 110 Hz is found in the convergence of biophysical values: a 110 Hz standing wave has a wave length equivalent to the average human skull (49.63 cm); the energy of this wave is within range of infrasonics capable of altering brain function ($3.5 \times 10\text{-}18$ J) ... 110 Hz can induce resonance in human vocal cords, and lowers left frontal activity while simultaneously increasing right temporal activity. 110 Hz is sufficient to stimulate Pacinian corpuscles [nerve endings in the skin responsible for sensitivity to vibration and pressure], can induce calcium efflux, and is a fundamental frequency of the hippocampus ... These results and quantitative support suggest that the rituals of prehistoric El Castillo utilized the natural resonance of the cave which enhanced a frequency with known neurological effects. These neurological effects are particularly salient with respect to sacred or neurotheological phenomena. (Gaona, Rouleau, et al. 2015)

SPECULATION

Regarding their resonance work at British and Irish Neolithic monuments, the ICRL team allowed itself some speculation concerning one of the Irish sites they tested – Newgrange. This site is a Neolithic chambered mound ("passage grave"), some 36ft (11m) high and 300ft (100m) in diameter. It is one of the greatest monuments of prehistory anywhere, and occupies a large bend in the river Boyne in County Meath, along with two companion

Figure 68. The spiral-carved entrance stone at Newgrange, Ireland.
(Note the vertical line at centre, possibly indicating the solar
alignment.) The roof box and passage entrance can be seen behind the
entrance stone. The rock slab to the right of the passage entrance is
thought to have been used like a door, to cover the entrance. If so, this
would have enhanced sounds made within the chamber.

chambered mounds, Dowth and the even larger Knowth, and
a variety of other smaller, earthen and megalithic monuments,
plus what had been a timber circle. (Aerial observations during
a heatwave in 2018 revealed crop marks showing the imprint of
what appears to once have been another great mound nearby.)

Around the base of Newgrange is kerbing comprised of 97
massive stones placed on edge, some of which are decorated with
carvings; in particular, lying across the mound's entrance is a
stone incised with a rich variety of spiral and lozenge designs.

The entrance gives access to a passage 62ft (18.9m) long
which leads to a corbelled stone chamber 20ft (6m) high, which
yielded a fundamental resonance cut almost precisely at 110
Hz. The chamber has three side-chambers or recesses, and large
stone basins were found in two of them. There is rock art in the

passage and in the chamber recesses, including a famous triple spiral carving.

Ringed by an incomplete circle of standing stones, Newgrange has been dated to around 3,200 B.C., making it older than Egypt's Great Pyramid, and is one of the oldest roofed structures in the world. It was known in Irish mythology as Bru na Boinne, the palace by the Boyne, and was where the ancient Lords of Light were said to dwell. This is a particularly appropriate legend because the monument's passage aligns to the rising midwinter sun, providing one of the most dramatic and best confirmed examples of ancient astronomy. The midwinter sunbeams stream through a special 'roof box' situated above the passage entrance and for a short while enter the chamber, making the stones there glow like copper ingots.

Figure 69. One of the large stone basins in a recess in the chamber at Newgrange.

Figure 70. Sunbeam shining down the entrance passage at
Newgrange. The passage rises to meet the floor of the chamber
(behind the camera position in this picture.)

Two blocks of quartz were filling the roof box when archaeologists first started excavating the site, but marks on the top of
the entrance lintel showed they had been removed and replaced
at various times, presumably in prehistory. Members of the ICRL
team assumed that this opening of the roof box would surely have
occurred at midwinter to allow in the sunbeam, perhaps for some
kind of solstitial ceremony. They wondered if a small group of
officiants, priests or shamans, would have gathered in the chamber
and intoned a deep continuous chant at a baritone frequency of
around 110Hz – perhaps something like Tibetan overtone chanting. If there was incense smoke in the chamber, or steam (there are
known Irish Iron Age sites, at least, that some have argued were
akin to Native American sweat lodges), the midwinter sunbeam
would have cut through it like a laser when it entered the chamber.

Because sound is a physical force, the floating particles in the smoke or steam would be organised into waveforms that would show up in the sunbeam – a sight that could perhaps even have inspired some of the zig-zag rock art in the chamber.

But could this sonic effect really have been physically possible? To laboratory test the idea, an acoustical device known as a Kundt's tube was used. Simply put, in the ICRL experiment this consisted of a transparent air-sealed tube with a light beam shining through it from one end and a sound generator at the other. Along the bottom of the tube was sprinkled a very fine dust (actually, mushroom spores). Sound was pumped into the tube until its resonant frequency was reached. Gradually, the spores rose up from the bottom of the tube and assembled themselves in the tube's still, sealed air into the wavelength pattern of the

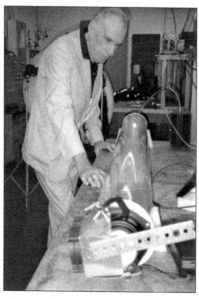

Figure 71. The late professor Robert Jahn with the Kundt's tube in the ICRL laboratory at Princeton University, which demonstrated that sound alone can move matter. [Photo: Arnold Lettieri/ICRL]

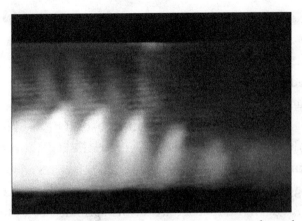

Figure 72. Sonically-levitated fungi spores organising themselves
to reveal standing waves of the acoustic resonance inside the
Kundt's tube (Photo: Arnold Lettieri/ICRL)

resonant, standing, soundwaves. It was a remarkable sight, to realise this was happening due purely to the energy of the sound. Whether or not the speculations about the Newgrange chamber and the midwinter sunbeam are correct, the experiment was a powerful reminder that sound is physical energy.

RINGING ROCKS

One of the more remarkable facts about rock acoustics is that some rocks, especially granitic ones, can produce musical sounds when struck with another, smaller rock ('hammerstone'). These are referred to as 'ringing rocks' or 'rock gongs', or, if with evidence of past human use, 'lithophones'. Such rocks are not exactly uncommon in some geological contexts, but they are sufficiently unusual to be noteworthy. To ancient peoples the sounds they produced must have seemed to be the music of the rock spirits, veritable fairy music.

The use of such sonorous rocks goes back at least as far as the Palaeolithic painted caves in France and Spain, those mysterious cavern systems whose walls were emblazoned tens of thousands of years ago with strange abstract markings and with images of bison, horses, sabre-toothed tigers, mammoth elephants and other creatures. It has been found that some of the stalactites, stalagmites and other calcite formations in these places produce musical sounds when struck lightly, sometimes even with a finger nail. The types of sounds produced range from pure bell-like ringing noises to melodious harp-like notes to gong-like tones (Dams 1985). Close examination of some of these calcite formations has revealed small-scale painted symbols and percussion marks so ancient they have been overlaid with translucent calcite deposits thousands of years old. So it is that some of the subterranean images in these Old Stone Age caverns had their own soundtracks, which we can still hear.

Stone Age usage of ringing and musical rocks is confirmed elsewhere. On the Karetski Peninsula that pokes its rocky finger into the eastern side of Lake Onega, north of St. Petersburg in Russia, there is a thick, flat rock that lies across a fissure that runs 33 feet (10m) down to the water. It is in a focus area of prehistoric rock carvings. When it is struck with a piece of wood the slab or rock emits a low bass sound that can be heard right across the peninsula, a distance of well over 2 miles (4km). Researchers think that the fissure or crack "conducts the sound to the lake and onto the surface of the water" (Lauhakangas 1999). Other ringing rocks used in prehistory are known of in Scotland, Scandinavia and elsewhere in Europe, and also in China, where ringing rocks were favoured for use in rock gardens (see below). But it is probably Africa where the greatest variety of lithophones was used culturally in prehistoric times. Examples are known of in Nigeria, Uganda, Tanzania, Kenya, and Sudan; ethnographic information indicates their use in rites of passage, fertility or rainmaking rituals, as signalling devices, and even for entertainment.

The pioneer of African research, and ringing rock research in general, was Bernard Fagg, who chronicled what he termed 'rock gongs' in the mid-20th Century. He particularly focused on Nigeria. At Birnin Kudu in Jigawa state, northern Nigeria, he found rock gongs clustered in the close vicinity of the Dutsen Abude caves which contain Neolithic rock art. He experimented with tuning forks to establish that the rock gongs had been carefully selected from the surrounding 2-square-mile ($5km^2$) scatter of granite outcrops so that an organised series of sounds could be produced. (One lithophone he measured yielded a fundamental frequency of 215 Hz at one of the depressions on its surface that had been formed by uncounted years of percussion.)

Fagg was also able to demonstrate that with a little practice local drummers could emulate the sounds of the full range of their tribal drums, including the hourglass-shaped 'talking drum' (*kalangu*), on the rock gongs (Fagg, 1956, 1956b, 1957). One might speculate, though, that perhaps the drums were developed to more conveniently emulate the ringing rock sounds!

Rock gongs have been noted in the Sudanese Nile valley, in particular from the Third and the Sixth Nile Cataracts, and more recently in several parts of the Fourth Cataract area. German researcher Cornelia Kleinitz studied the lithophones on Ishashi Island at the Fourth Cataract, ahead of flooding produced by the creation of the controversial Merowe Dam, which was inaugurated in 2009. She found twenty-five rock gongs and seventeen complexes of them in the granitic landscape, showing various intensities of percussion markings on them. Kleinitz felt it to be likely that "activities at the different rock gong phenomena had diverse motivations and were directed at different audiences"

(Kleinitz 2003-4). The lithophones were virtually all found in association with Neolithic carvings of cattle in the rock art of the area. Where carvings were actually on a lithophone, the tones produced by the rocks were of a notably bell-like nature. Because of the variety of tones the various lithophones produced, Kleinitz considers that "not only rhythms, but proper melodies may have been played". Noting that the current inhabitants of the area now know nothing about the origins or purposes of lithophones, she aptly observes that "the soundscape of Ishashi thus went out of use well before the modern era".

It might be that knowledge of ringing granite found greater sophistication further down the Nile in Egypt. For instance, there is a fallen obelisk in the great temple complex of Karnak in Luxor. If the ear is placed close to the pyramidal point and the block struck with the hand, the whole piece of cut granite can be heard to resonate. Goethe referred to architecture as "frozen music" and so it seems it could have literally been the case in ancient Egypt: did the temples of the Nile have their own sacred notes, their own sonic frequencies?

In ancient Greece such sonic phenomena were certainly noted, as the travel writer, Pausanias, indicated in the second century A.D. He reported on the belief of the citizens of the city of Megara in Attica, Greece, that the god Apollo helped to build the walls of the Alkathous acropolis there. In order to free his hands, Apollo laid his lyre down on a stone. Ever since, "if anyone chances to hit the stone with a pebble, it sounds exactly like a lyre that is struck", Pausanias reported (*Description of Greece 1. 42. 2*). Along with colleagues, I checked out the site, to see if we could identify the Lyre Stone, but unfortunately the temple site has now been destroyed and its construction materials cannibalised for later buildings – it is just possible the musical stone is lodged anonymously and mutely somewhere in the walls of one of the stone-built houses that now stand on the site.

Hints abound indicating that the knowledge and usage of lithophones was widespread in the ancient world. Take the ancient, now ruined city of Jeresh in Jordan, a place occupied since Neolithic times. Amidst its paved and colonnaded streets, plazas, towers and gates, there is a set of lithophones. That these are not accidental inclusions is demonstrated by the fact that the tones they produce are scaled, but at what point in the long history of Jeresh they were used remains to be determined.

But nowhere was lithophonic sophistication more pronounced than in ancient India.

Temple lithophones in ancient India

In 2002, archaeologist Nicole Boivin, then of Cambridge University, and Ravi Korisettar of Karnataka University led an archaeological team that rediscovered Neolithic rock art on the multi-peaked, granitic Kupgal Hill in the Bellary District of India's southern Deccan. There are hundreds of rock engravings, mainly of long-horned cattle, interspersed with some human figures. While studying and recording the imagery, the team was informed by local people that among the rock art there were rocks that made deep, gong-like noises when struck. This was demonstrated for the archaeologists who marvelled at the sounds the rocks produced. Some of the lithophones had round depressions where percussion had occurred over long periods of time. (Boivin 2004, and personal communication.)

What is most interesting, though, is that only about 50 miles away is the temple complex of Hampi (the ancient royal city of Vijayanagara), and at least one of the temples there, notably the

Figure 73. The ringing rocks on Kupgal Hill, Bellary District, India. See text. [Photo: Courtesy N. Boivin]

medieval Vittala temple, contains granitic musical stone pillars erected thousands of years after the rock art on Kupgal Hill had been carved. There are 56 musical pillars at the temple known as the 'SaRiGaMa Pillars', referencing four of the seven musical notes of classical Indian Music. The pillars produce musical tones when tapped, ranging from drum-like sounds to bell-like tones, and that is by no means the end of the sonic ingenuity displayed by the builders of this place.

Other temples further afield in southern India, notably in Tamil Nadu, also possess musical stone pillars; Nellaiyapper temple, for instance, where columns fashioned out of a single block of rock fourteen hundred years ago are able to issue basic notes of classical Indian music when struck. Again, the multi-period Meenakshi Amman Temple in Madurai houses among its halls

Figure 74. The musical pillars (the thinner ones) in Vijaya Vittala
Temple, Hampi, India. [Photo: Vinayak Kulkarni/Wikimedia
Commons/CC BY-SA 3.0]

the so-called Thousand Pillar Hall (16th Century). Not only are
the pillars lithophones, the hall itself is apparently skillfully built to
be anechoic. (In addition to such acoustic mysteries the positioning of the pillars is a geometrically arranged visual marvel.) Keen
to promote it as a tourist attraction, the Tamil Nadu tourist people
refer to it as "The greatest musical instrument in the world".

There are at the very least a dozen other Indian temples where
lithophonic rocks are involved, and it is clear that a sophisticated acoustic technology using rocks developed over thousands of
years from the Neolithic era to the early and late medieval periods
in India.

Bayinshi

In China, rocks were thought to be concentrations of the Earth's
invisible energy, *chi* (*qi* in Japanese), the secret animating force of
the world, and rocks of unusual shapes or properties were consid-

ered to be especially endowed with it. Just being near to such powerful rocks could have a beneficial effect on a person's flow of *chi* and therefore health and state of mind. Some rocks were bought and sold on account of their powerful qualities, and it was not unknown for a person to become awed and reverential when encountering an especially strong rock. The 8th-century scholar and politician, Li Deyu, built a celebrated rock garden near Luoyang, a major Chinese city and site of the first Buddhist temple in China. He used rocks selected from specific locations around the country, including from Lake Tai (Taihu), west of Shanghai. Rocks from this lake – which apparently may have originated as a meteoric crater – were highly prized on two counts: they tended to be weirdly shaped giving rise to simulacra of miniature mountains and landscapes and, often, when struck, they could give off a sound – "Their ringing resonance clearer than jasper chimes" as the poet Bai Juyi (A.D. 772-846), described it.

Such lithophones were known as "resonant rocks" (*bayinshi*), another prime example being the finely textured 'Lingbi' rocks from the Stone Chime Mountains in Jiangxi Province. "The best Chinese rock will sound as well as look impressive when tapped," art historian Francoise Berthier informs (Berthier 2000).

In the Americas

The fascination with and use of ringing rocks was worldwide, so we can expect to find them in the Americas too. In fact, it is where we find what is possibly the only natural lithophone openly featured in a museum – the Bowers Museum in Santa Ana, California. There, the seven-ton Bell Rock sits on a concrete plinth in the entrance courtyard. Hollows where percussion had taken place over unknown centuries are visible on its upper

Figure 75. Bell Rock, Bowers Museum, Santa Ana, California. *Top*: General view. *Bottom*: Close-up of percussion hollows on the rock's surface.

surface. The great granite boulder had been brought down from Bell Canyon many years ago after vandals had toppled it from its position perched on smaller rocks. Like all lithophones, it needed air space around it in order to resonate properly, but now it rests mute on its concrete base in the museum's grounds.

There are numerous known rocks in southern California that still ring (see site example below).

Why do some rocks ring?

It is claimed that geological analysis of the pillars at Hampi has shown that the rocks are resonant partially because they contain large amounts of silica, but in truth the precise reasons ringing rocks in general ring still seems to be subject to varied opinions. They are usually granitic (though not always – for instance, the Taihu rocks in China derive from geologically ancient deposits of limestone) and so are likely to contain considerable amounts of crystalline material, such as feldspar, which is what gives the term 'spotted' to the spotted dolerite of the Carn Menyn bluestone.

The presence of iron in some rocks does not seem to be a special factor in their sonorous qualities. It has also been suggested that the crystalline structure constituting rocks that ring are those that possess a more than usual amount of internal stress, resulting in a dynamic tension analogous to the way a guitar string can be made to produce various musical tones when it is stretched to various degrees. The size and shape of rocks do not necessarily indicate whether or not they are 'ringers', but all sonorous stones do need some air space around them to allow them to resonate, or else their ringing properties are severely damped or totally muted.

There has been very little scientific study of the acoustic frequencies of ringing rocks when tapped, and because there is so much variability there probably wouldn't be much point in doing so. In broad experiential terms, ringing rocks' sounds can be likened to bells, drums (especially tin drums), deep gong-like tones, harps, or harsh metallic hammer-on-anvil types of sound.

SITE EXAMPLES

Hebridean ringing rocks

Near Balaphetrish on the Scottish Inner Hebridean island of Tiree, there is a remote boulder some 10 feet (3m) across that issues clear metallic sounds when struck with a small hammer-stone. It is a presumed glacial erratic, because it is not native to the island's geology. The rock is covered with over fifty round depressions – some of these could be original Neolithic cup-mark rock art, but most, certainly the larger ones, are where the boulder has been struck repeatedly over untold generations. It was clearly

Figure 76. The Balaphetrish ringing rock, Tiree, Scotland.

Figure 77. The Iona lithophone and its hammerstone in its specially-carved niche.

singled out as a lithophone long ago by the island's inhabitants. The rock has folklore attached to it and offerings were made at it in the form of coins deposited on its top surface.

There is a lesser-known ringing rock on the holy island of Iona, also in the Scottish Inner Hebrides. It sits on the eastern coast of the island: although now rarely visited, it was obviously once a noted feature because a deep hollow was carved on it to hold a hammerstone – the one nested there now is probably not the original. The story of this sonorous rock is seemingly unknown; it may have been used way back in the Bronze Age, or in the early medieval period by monks – Iona was a major monastic centre of Celtic Christianity, said to have been founded by St Columba in the 6th Century. (The sounds of these two particular lithophones can be heard on the 'Audio Clips' page of the Dragon Project Trust website: http://dragonprojecttrust.org/audioclips.)

There are similar sorts of lithophonic rocks elsewhere in Scotland, and in Norway and Sweden (Hultman 2010, 2014;

Lund 2019), and doubtless across other parts of Europe, many with their own lore relating to spirits or magical powers.

Zion Wash vision quest site

At a remote Native American vision quest site in the Chuckwalla Mountains close to the Southern California - Mexico border, there is a slab of rock that rings with a pure metallic sound when struck with a small stone. On the top surface of the slab there is a rock-art glyph estimated to be c.1500 years old: it is an amorphous shape with one extension reaching towards the (well used) edge of the rock where the clearest sound can be produced. It may have been a functional indicator or the representation of the slab's indwelling spirit, but either way the lithophone was singled out and marked long ago. Its sound permeates the silence of the surrounding wilderness, and one can only imagine how it must have affected the altered mind state of a shaman or

Figure 78. The author striking the rock-art-marked ringing rock at Zion Wash, Southern California.

Figure 79. The calcite formation known as 'The Organ',
Nerja, Spain. [Courtesy Lya Dams]

rite-of-passage brave going days and nights without food or sleep
in order to have a vision.

Nerja, Spain

In the 1980s, the Belgian archaeologist Lya Dams conducted a
detailed study of some of the painted Palaeolithic caves of France
and the Iberian Peninsula. She was specifically looking for lithophones, and her starting point was the Spanish cave system of
Nerja, not far from Malaga (Dams 1984). The caverns there are
lofty with excellent acoustics, and occupation deposits have been
unearthed dating back to c.10,000 B.C. At the time of her investigation, nineteen paintings had been recorded within the cave,
but she went on to itemise some five hundred other figures, the
majority of them painted abstract markings or images in red or
black, and a few engravings. Animal figures are scarce. Nerja's
lithophone is called 'The Organ' and is a recess or 'sanctuary'
consisting of a triangular platform with a steep bank on one side
and, on the other, a wall of tightly-packed fluted calcite folds or

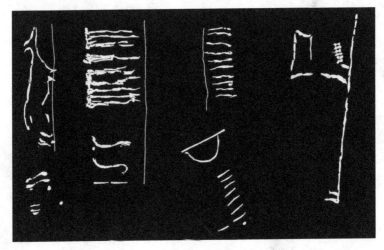

Figure 80. Palaeolithic markings amidst the calcite folds of The Organ
in the Nerja cave. [After Lya Dams]

'draperies' some 5 metres (16ft) in length and 4 metres (13ft) in height. These calcite folds have been tilted at an angle of 45 degrees due to earthquake activity in the past.

To reach this feature, the users of the cave during the Stone Age would have to have climbed over several huge boulders from the bottom of the main cavern, from which the Organ is not visible. An abstract sign, which Dams called the "beckoning sign", is found on a stalagmitic pillar on the approach to the Organ recess – and it is the only sign that can be seen from any sort of distance. Various sounds can be elicited from the calcite folds when their edges are struck with a hard object. Dams' team experimented with blunt flints and wooden sticks, the latter working best, to produce clear, harp-like notes which reverberated to the rear of the cave. It was noted that several of the calcite edges had been intentionally broken at various heights in ancient times, probably to vary the sounds. The edges of the folds have a worn appearance indicating percussive usage over a considerable time period.

The Organ is both visually and acoustically impressive. Dams' examination of the feature confirmed claims by an earlier antiquarian that there were paintings on it – many tucked away in the grooves between the folds. There were dozens of signs and markings – dots, strokes, spirals – and a small number of representational images, including a hind seemingly climbing up one of the calcite 'drapes'. It was clear that these paintings in red and black were not meant for display, but were more likely to have been adornments of a feature to which the cave users had obviously attached great importance, for the cave-artists did their work at this place without regard to visibility or easy access. Some of the markings started a height in excess of 2 metres (over 6 feet) from the ground, and when she was recording them Dams found herself using artificial toe-holes to reach the images, holes that must have been made by the original artists.

Figure 81. Mazinaw Rock, Bon Echo Park, Ontario, Canada.

Figure 82. Two examples of Mazinaw rock paintings. Painted in red
ochre, they are now very faded.

Mazinaw Rock, Bon Echo Park, Ontario, Canada

Mazinaw Rock, which is actually a cliff face created on a fault line, rises out of Mazinaw Lake and extends for a full mile (1.7km) at an average height of 100 feet (30m).

Panels of rock paintings run along the base of the cliff a little above the waterline; they were painted using red ochre (itself considered a sacred mineral) which is now somewhat faded. The imagery mainly consists of abstract markings but interspersed among these there are some figurative forms, including the large-eared jackrabbit spirit, Nanabush, and human-like beings in a canoe, usually the sign of spirits in American Indian rock art. This site is within Bon Echo Provincial Park, so named because the cliff-face produces remarkable echoes. (In summer, boat trips are given on the lake so visitors can experience the power of the Mazinaw echoes.) The rock panels cluster where the echoes are strongest.

The Carn Menyn Ridge, Preseli, Wales: A soundscape for Stonehenge?

In 2006, a research team from the Royal College of Art, London, initiated a detailed audio-visual study of Mynydd Preseli, in Wales (Devereux and Wozencoft 2014). The project was entitled 'Landscape-Perception', and its objective was to try to look at and listen to a relatively unspoiled prehistoric landscape as if with Stone Age eyes and ears, and Mynydd Preseli provided such a landscape. This upland is a rugged, wild tract punctuated by the looming, phantasmagorical forms of jumbled spotted dolerite outcrops. The igneous outcrops on and around the Carn Menyn ridge have been identified as the source area of at least some of the Stonehenge bluestones (the shorter standing stones at the monument).

Figure 83. A general view of the Carn Menyn ridge (middle distance, in sunlight) in the Preseli Hills (Mynydd Preseli) of South Wales, the source area of the Stonehenge bluestones. The three main rock outcrops can be seen on the ridge – there are other outcrops elsewhere on and around the ridge that are not visible in this view.

Petrological and geochemical analyses show that at least some of the Stonehenge bluestones (a collective term for dolerites, rhyolites, and tuffs) originated in the outcrops that form the Preseli ridge of Carn Menyn along with some of the surrounding carns (Thomas 1923; Thorpe et al. 1991; Ixer 1996; Williams-Thorpe et al. 2006; Darvill 2006). Most recently, an outcrop immediately below the western end of the ridge, Carn Goedog (pronounced 'goy-doch'), has been claimed as a major source (Bevins, Ixer and Pearce 2013.)

Although this project was essentially an art-based study, aimed at getting art students to engage with landscape in an unfiltered, direct way, the fact of the Carn Menyn ridge being the principal source area of many of the Stonehenge bluestones gave an archaeological aspect to the enterprise. As the concern here is with sound, the visual findings made by the project are omitted and focus put only on the acoustic aspect.

The ringing property of Preseli stones in general had been signalled in the 1950s by the indefatigable rock-gong hunter, Bernard Fagg, and he noted that the name of a Preseli village, Maenclochog, was Welsh for "ringing stones" or "bell stones". The place was so named because instead of church bells it had two rocks that rang like bells (apparently, the rocks were destroyed in the 18th Century). So, over dozens of field trips during a seven-year period, the project's researchers, using small hammerstones, conducted organised transects across the Carn Menyn ridge percussion-testing well over a thousand rocks in order to obtain a clearer picture of the incidence of 'ringers' along the ridge.

Overall, the project found a 5-10 percent general occurrence of ringing rocks on and around the ridge, which is quite significant, but in localised areas, especially those suspected of being Neolith-

Figure 84. Bluestones are the shorter ones at Stonehenge, and were the first, original, stones at the site. Here we see four of them (one fallen on the left in this view, and note the damaged corners of the standing bluestones.). The larger sarsen stones are relatively local and were erected much later on.

Figure 85. Part of Carn Goedog, Preseli, claimed by experts to be the
main source of the Stonehenge bluestones.

ic quarry sites, the incidence level rose by two or three times. As a
point of interest, Carn Goedog was found to contain a high propor-
tion of ringing rocks. What was particularly noted was that when a
Goedog ringer was struck, its metallic sound travelled a considerable distance. (As this book was in production, new research reported
that bluestones from Goedog originally were used to form a huge
stone circle at a fairly nearby site on Preseli called Waun Mawr.
According to the research, these stones were later transported to
Stonehenge as part of the initial construction of that famous site.
If correct, this would seemingly make Stonehenge a second-hand
monument! The research was published in *Antiquity*: M. Parker
Pearson et al., vol. 95, no. 379, February 2021. This was followed up
by a BBC documentary on 12 February 2021.)

Of course, identifying a ringing rock today does not necessarily mean it was recognised as such in prehistory. In other
words, intention cannot be demonstrated. It turned out, howev-

er, that archaeologists Wainwright and Darvill (the latter being an archaeological adviser to the project) had identified a couple of instances of prehistoric rock art on or around the ridge. One of these examples was of particular interest to the Landscape Perception study: it was probably a fallen standing stone at a now dried-up spring on the southern slope of the Carn Menyn ridge. The stone was found by our Landscape-Perception project researchers to be a ringer. But more importantly, it was indented with a line of six cup marks. There is no way anyone could have produced these without appreciating that the stone produced a metallic sound. It was a lithophone. In any case, there can be little doubt that the Neolithic inhabitants or visitors to this area would not have failed to notice how many rocks were sonorous.

It was obvious that eventually the project would have to visit Stonehenge to study the bluestones in situ at the monument. In 2013, project members tested all the bluestones now standing at

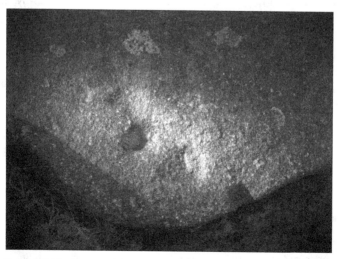

Figure 86. The cup-marked ringing stone on Carn Menyn, proving that the Neolithic people there recognised the sound from stones. [Photo: Sol Devereux]

Stonehenge. Unfortunately, none of them rang out clearly – as discussed earlier, ringing rocks need to have air space around them to properly resonate, but all the Stonehenge bluestones are fixed in the ground, mainly in concrete bases, so any ringing capacity is severely damped. Nevertheless, at least a hint of resonance was detected in a few cases. What was noticed in close inspection of the bluestones, though, was clear visual evidence that the corners of many of them had been struck at some remote point in the past (see Figure 84). It is impossible to say whether or not this was damage caused in transit, or pieces being knocked off by people thinking the stones had magical or healing qualities, or by ritualists striking the stones to make them ring (perhaps before they began their long journey from Preseli, or some other point en route), like Aladdin rubbing the lamp to make the genie appear.

It is known that during the Stone Age 'pieces of places' were circulated as relics, in which material from venerated natural locations was transported to other, usually monumental, sites, often far away. These 'pieces' might be in the form of polished ritual hand-axes or else as rocks or clay to add to monuments that were being built – for example, the quartz in the mighty Newgrange Neolithic monument in Ireland was brought from the Wicklow Hills some 60 miles (97km) distant. In the case of Stonehenge, we see, suitable pillar-shaped bluestones were prised from the Preseli outcrops and transported to Salisbury Plain, roughly 190 miles (300km) away by land. They were among the first stones to be erected at the Stonehenge site, which already existed as an earthwork. The abiding mystery has been *why* these Preseli bluestones, weighing several tons apiece, were transported to Stonehenge. What power, what *mana* or perceived special power did they possess? In conducting their project, the Royal College of Art investigators may possibly have chanced upon an unexpected answer – the Carn Menyn area turns out to be a soundscape.

There is no doubt that the Preseli upland as a whole was already highly venerated, as is testified by the numerous megalithic monuments scattered through and around the hill range. Did the builders of Stonehenge believe, like the American Indians and the Bushmen of southern Africa, or members of the indigenous Shinto religion in Japan, that spirits or magical power resided within the singing rocks? Was that what made the bluestones special?

Bryn Celli Ddu, Anglesey, Wales

Bryn Celli Ddu is a Neolithic mound containing a stone chamber on the island of Anglesey, off the north coast of Wales. It comprises a passage and a sub-circular chamber set within a circular ditch. The mound is 26m (85ft) in diameter, but originally may have been larger.

There is a free-standing monolith inside the chamber, and, found outside the mound during excavation, was an abstractly decorated stone known as the Pattern Stone.

Figure 87. The entrance to the Neolithic passage grave of Bryn Celli Ddu.

The monument stands in a complex sacred geography, which, as I discovered, has a sonic component to it. A percussive sound (such as handclapping) made at the site produces a distinctive point echo from the surrounding landscape.

It turned out that the point source of the echo was the broad face of a lone rock outcrop about 145m (476ft) to the north of Bryn Celli Ddu. Could this be simply a coincidence?

That seems less likely, because the reflective side of the outcrop is marked with prehistoric cup-marks. This distinctive echo from a rock outcrop that was so clearly marked out in Neolithic times is suggestive of the possibility that the acoustic connection between the monument and the natural rock feature is more than merely accidental. It would be unlikely that Stone Age ears would have failed to notice the echo.

We need to be mindful that certain natural features were themselves venerated in ancient times (Tilley 1994; Whitley 1994; Bradley 2000; Devereux 2000) and especially natural rocks that produced sounds in one way or another – ringers or producers of distinctive echoes (DuBois 1908; Fagg 1957; Berthier 1989; Fagg 1997; Boivin 2004; Loose 2008). This related to cross-cultural beliefs around the ancient world we've referred to previously

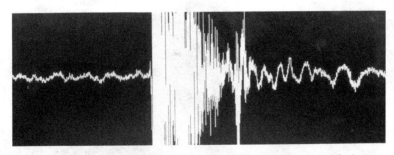

Figure 88. A sound trace of the point echo. The handclap is seen as the large focus of waves and the echo is represented by the spike shortly following it (to the right).

Figure 89. The naked eye view of the outcrop from the monument. Its distinct flat face is clearly evident.

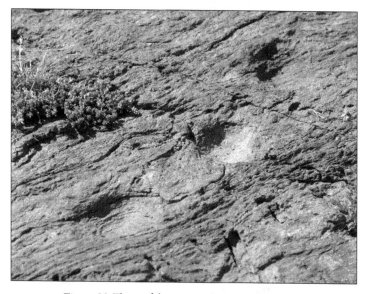

Figure 90. Three of the cup-markings on the outcrop.
[Photo: George Nash]

that spirits or supernatural forces existed behind or within rock surfaces and cliff faces (Dowson and Lewis-Williams 1989; Rajnovich 1994; Whitley 1996; Dowson 1998; Lewis-Williams 2002; Levin and Suzukei 2006; Lewis-Williams and Loubser 2014). So in the case of Bryn Celli Ddu, we might surmise that the echoing rock outcrop was viewed as special or sacred long before the building of the monument itself took place.

PART TWO

OTHER KINDS OF POWER

Section Introduction

There can be powers – or qualities or properties, call them what you will – of ancient sites other than purely physical energies. Because of its limited resources, the Dragon Project Trust focused mainly on monitoring measurable energies, but even in its early phase (late 1970s to mid-1980s) it wanted to extend its investigations beyond just physical energies, to tentatively begin exploring how the human mind and body interacted with sacred place. So it introduced a very modest side-programme making on-site studies with people claiming skills in dowsing and psychical abilities, which was lumped together as 'primary sensing'. Such efforts were limited primarily to the Rollright Stones complex. We wanted to know if such primary sensing could tell us anything reliable about the complex. The final form of primary sensing detailed in this segment is *sensory archaeology*. This is now entering the fold of acceptable mainstream archaeology and has twin tracks – technical and phenomenological ones. Here in this section we will focus on the latter – the study of archaeological sites with the bodily senses.

From the early 1990s, the DPT took on a highly nuanced and hugely controversial avenue of enquiry, one that asked if the *dreaming mind* could access, or notice, information at a site that bypassed waking awareness. This approach was based on the very ancient practice of temple sleep. Because of its logistically demanding nature, the programme progressed only in fits and starts for fully a decade.

Both these programmes are detailed further in their respective chapters in the following pages. The final chapter of this section, however, takes us to something beyond any kind of organised enquiry or response to sacred place – *numinosity*, an intangible sense of 'atmosphere' or 'spirit of place'. It is the most profound kind of 'power' of certain ancient and sacred places, but like consciousness itself, everyone feels it without necessarily being openly aware of it or fully understanding what it is – as we shall discuss.

5

PRIMARY SENSING

The term 'primary sensing' can encapsulate a wide and diverse range of phenomenological approaches, including fresh, insightful, visual and other sensory observations, subtle bodily reactions, mental intuitions, and more. By their very nature, such approaches tend to get derided or overlooked because most of them cannot always be objectively confirmed as actual or, at least, significant to the accepted mainstream process of research. Yet they can sometimes yield additional information about a site, or lead to more concrete findings. Indeed, I suspect more 'objective research' owes its springboard to an initial phenomenological stimulus than might readily be admitted to.

In this chapter, we will look at just a short set of examples of various kinds of primary sensing, starting with probably the best-known form of apparent subtle bodily reaction – dowsing.

DOWSING

Also known as water-divining or water-witching, dowsing is a form of divination using a suitable hand-held implement to amplify minor muscle twitches that are said to occur in the dowser when he or she locates a subterranean target. The method is primarily used on-site, finding subterranean water sources or channels, metal deposits and lost objects, although it has other claimed applications as well.

The traditional dowsing tool is a flexible Y-branched twig – typically hazel, but not necessarily so – which bends up or down when a target has been reached. Towards the end of the 19th Century, the pendulum (any small suitably weighty object tied to a length of thread) started to be used as well. Nowadays there are all kinds of dowsing gadgets; probably the most popular being the angle rods – lengths of wire (such as from wire coat hangers), bent in a right angle, one end held lightly or inserted in a sleeve that is held in the hand. If the rod swings, or, if a pair is used, when the rods cross over each other, the dowser assumes he or she is walking over the underground target. Some dowsers do not use devices at all, holding their hands in such a way that they can feel the slight reactions in them as they pass over a target location.

It is possible that dowsing in some form or other has been practiced since very early times, but apart from some debatable evidence for it in ancient China, one of the first securely documented historical accounts of the method being used is in a 16th–century German book on mining called the *De Re Metallica*. Although the book's author, Georgius Agricola, expressed skepticism about the method, something made the Germans into the best miners and mineralogists of their day. This and other early historical references are to dowsing as a means of prospecting for minerals. One of the first mentions of water dowsing as such was provided by the English antiquarian John Aubrey in the latter part of the 17th Century, when he reported that "water may be found by a divining rod made of willowe".

Dowsing has had a conceptual association with megaliths that goes back to at least the 1930s, when French dowsers claimed that standing stones were positioned over the crossing of subterranean streams. This was noted in England just before World War II by dowser archaeologist Reginald a Smith. Around the same time, German dowsers ('radiesthesiasts') began reporting that they could detect harmful radiation issuing from the ground, and some claimed there were grids of such energy spread over the entire globe. After the war, British dowser Guy Underwood picked up on Smith's rendering of the French work, and proceeded to develop a complex theory that involved underground streams beneath megalithic sites and old churches. He hypothesized that dowsing had been part of "prehistoric religions". When his book, *The Pattern of the Past*, was published posthumously in 1969, it had a great impact on the new generation of populist ancient mysteries enthusiasts.

This linked in to a growing popular belief that unspecified but dowsable energies ran along 'ley lines', with prehistoric sites and other ancient structures being nodes of said energies. This idea was, in fact, first postulated by a dowser, Arthur Lawton, in the 1930s, but really exploded into a dominant notion among populist ancient mysteries enthusiasts in the 1960s, and has proliferated ever since, largely due to the internet, and has become ever more fantastical. Aided and abetted by websites, popular TV shows, and a plethora of books and magazine articles, it now spawns notions of planetary energy grids, terrestrial acupuncture points, shimmering geometrical energy patterns embedded in the ground, and similar. None of it is accountable in any objective way, so has become fantasizing untethered to any evidential objectivity.

As we have noted (Part One) the popular beliefs in, or rumours of energies at ancient sites, from old folklore to modern-day claims were a reason the DPT was established in the first place, to see if some objective evidence could be found for the persistent rumour. Hence the monitoring of physical energies. In the same vein, it was thought that the DPT should at least take a look at dowsing, so enmeshed had it become with claims of 'energies'.

Now, no one working on the DPT, including myself, had any doubts that in some cases dowsing, when conducted by consistently successful practitioners, could be effective – after all, it was accountable: either water, metal, or lost objects were found, or not. I well recall being on a farm in Wales during a serious drought in 1976, when the farmers told me that they were using the best "dowser in the valley" to sink temporary wells. It was practical, it worked, and none of the farmers thought anything unusual about it. Likewise, there are even specialist archaeological dowsers who are sometimes used in tasks such as finding underground foundations of ancient buildings to guide excavation – though their role is now being made somewhat redundant with aerial observation and new geophysical methods of mapping underground features. On the other hand, the more extreme claims of so-called 'energy dowsing' have no solid objective evidential basis at all.

During the DPT's work in this field, a number of dowsers were invited individually on site at the King's Men circle and other components of the Rollright Stones. Could an accountable way of using dowsing be found? The dowsers were brought on site at different times, so reducing the chance of there being unintentional collusion regarding results. Each was given identical site plans on which to mark their dowsing findings at three designated levels beneath the ground. The DPT wanted to see if individual dowsers, on totally separate occasions, would produce results that roughly corresponded with one another. It didn't happen. But there were a few isolated results of some interest.

A leading British dowser (who wished to remain anonymous) was one of those invited to conduct a dowsing survey. He had thirteen dowsing reactions inside the stone circle he described as "small areas with points of force in them ... I have no proof of what these are, but for the moment I think they must be particles

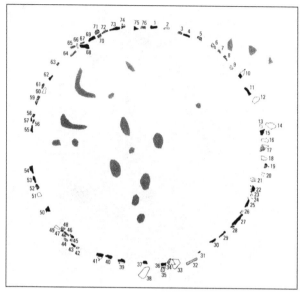

Figure 91. The areas of tone represent magnetic anomalies within Rollright's King's Men circle. [Derived from a magnetic survey by English Heritage]

of meteorite that has struck the ground and buried themselves". Interestingly, English Heritage (now called Heritage England) had previously conducted a magnetic survey in and around the King's Men circle. They recorded fourteen magnetic anomaly spots within the ring of stones. These could have been caused by a number of factors, such as patches of burning, buried tree stumps, rocks, or indeed, buried fragments of meteorite. With regard to the dowsing reactions it does not matter, it is just intriguing that there was a close correspondence between the dowsing reactions and the magnetic anomaly spots.

Another of the invited dowsers was the Welsh Master dowser, the late Bill Lewis, who had a sparkling record of various successes using his primary sensing, which included not only standard dowsing, but also finding lost people, aiding police

Figure 92. Welsh master dowser, Bill Lewis, dowsing at the
King's Men circle, Rollright, using angle rods.

work, and what might be called 'psychic healing' – sometimes
referred to as the 'laying on of hands'. When he dowsed, he used
a chart showing the electromagnetic spectrum, and he selected
which frequency he would be dowsing. He was very meticulous.

One of the abilities he had demonstrated at a number of
megaliths around the country was to dowse what he called "energy
nodes" at particular points on standing stones. On one occasion
he was filmed dowsing the nodes on a megalith at Crickhowell in
Wales (Hitching 1976). A physicist then scanned the stone with a
magnetometer and the needle on the instrument flickered significantly every time the probe passed over one of Lewis's dowsed
nodes. So we asked him to do the same thing during his Rollright
work. He selected the tallest (northernmost) stone in the circle.
This was connected to a sensitive voltmeter situated several
metres away by means of a cable. It was measuring the millivolt-

age in the stone and was giving a virtually steady reading. The end of the cable was taped to the stone about four-fifths up its height just below the point where Lewis dowsed one of his energy nodes. Every time Lewis laid his hands on the node (not on the end of the cable), the readings on the voltmeter strongly reacted. The effect was repeated time and again.

Sceptics on site felt that anyone placing their hands at the point on the stone would cause the effect, but when this was tested multiple times no one else could affect the instrument's readings. It was then suggested that perhaps coincidental lightning in some distant thunder storm was inducing an electrical effect in the cable connecting the stone and the voltmeter. We had an electrostatic detector on site, so this suggestion was tested. There was no correlation between any bursts of distant static and Lewis's actions.

Figure 93. Bill Lewis (centre) affects the voltage in a monitored Rollright stone. John Steele, a Dragon Project co-ordinator in the early phase of the project, looks on.

This was one of the first glimmers of objectivity with regard to on-site energy dowsing, because, overall, this short and limited test of dowsing during the primary sensing programme of the Project wasn't found to be a great success. But hints like this result cry out for more prolonged and objective studies.

Psychic archaeology

Many of us at one time or another will no doubt have stood within some ancient ruins or prehistoric site and tried to picture in our mind's eye what went on there in remote antiquity. At various points during the 20th Century this urge took on a more structured form, if it can be so called, that eventually became known as "psychic archaeology". One of the more celebrated early cases of this involved the architect Frederick Bligh Bond and his investigations of medieval Glastonbury Abbey in Somerset, southern England. Bond had been appointed director of excavations at the ruined abbey site and he began work with psychic mediums who had the claimed ability to write down "spirit messages" while supposedly in trance, a process known as automatic writing. In the course of numerous sittings between 1907 and 1912, Bond had amassed information in Latin, Middle English and modern English purporting to come from long-dead monks associated with Glastonbury. Architectural information regarding the site was offered in this manner, and Bond was apparently able to confirm some of this material by his excavations. In his *The Gate of Remembrance* (1918), Bond unwisely revealed the unconventional source of his excavational guidance, and this had unfortunate consequences for him professionally. Bond kept an open mind as to whether the communications were from the dead or from some form of "greater memory" belonging to the human race as a whole, a concept in keeping with C.G. Jung's theory of the Collective Unconscious, and with the occult idea of the 'Akashic Records'.

In the decades between the World Wars it became quite the fashion among some investigators to invite psychic sensitives to ancient sites to see what they could 'see' or sense – a form of claimed psychism known as, 'psychometry' when applied to places or objects. Two sensitives particularly noted for this kind of thing at the time were Geraldine Cummins and Iris Campbell. At the Irish stone circle of Drumbeg, Cummins claimed her inner eye could look back in time and see "earth power" being drawn from the ground by robed officiants and used for what she termed a low, elemental form of magic.

Campbell also felt that the stones of Long Meg and her Daughters, a major megalithic site in the English Lake District, formed a "receiving station" for "earth vibrations" and could be used for the transmission of messages by pressing one's palms against them. Another site, Mayburgh Henge near Penrith in northern England,

Figure 94. Drumbeg stone circle, Ireland.

was, according to her, "an experimental area ... where magnetism was induced from the four points of the compass", whatever that meant.

Such psychics were frequently employed by John Foster Forbes, a Scottish antiquarian with occult tastes. He believed that the megaliths had been placed by survivors from Atlantis and that quartz in the stones was used variously to attract telluric (ground) currents and, at certain times, cosmic forces.

In later times, a number of American investigators of ancient sites also tried employing psychics. Jeffrey Goodman, in his influential book *Psychic Archaeology* (1977), described exceptionally vivid dreams in which he saw a place apparently in the American Southwest where he uncovered archaeological evidence of previously unsuspected early human presence on the continent. These dreams led him to contact a psychic call Aaron Abrahamson who obtained information, he claimed, by accessing a universal psychic record, receiving messages from discarnate spirits, and by employing clairvoyance – or remote viewing as it is usually called nowadays. By these means Goodman eventually located the place he had seen in his dreams near Flagstaff, Arizona.

Over the same general period, another set of investigators called the Mobius Group, founded by Stephan Schwartz, made use of apparently accurate psychics – Hella Hamid and George McMullen – in remote viewing to guide archaeological excavations to uncover hitherto undiscovered sites in Egypt.

In *The Ancient Stones Speak* (1979), archaeological explorer David Zink describes using a number of psychics to enhance his visits to a selected range of sacred sites worldwide. For instance, according to one of Zink's psychic allies, the megalithic site of Callanish on Scotland's Isle of Skye was built to communicate with the Pleiades constellation in some way, and the energies created at the site "disoriented many". Another sensitive divined that the Neolithic site of Ḥaġar Qim on Malta "served one purpose ... communion with extra-terrestrial beings". As might be expected, Egypt's Great Pyramid brought forth a rich crop of claimed psychic impressions, including that it was an "energy collector and beacon", its stones could trigger out-of-body experiences, and (of course!) that it had been built by survivors of Atlantis.

At the present day, similar sorts of claims proliferate. Like most 'fringe' research areas, unless psychic archaeology produces tangible, excavational evidence (which it sometimes does), it will lack any objective frame of reference, and fantasy gets included with possibly interesting material. There is no wise reason to automatically reject the possibility of *psi* (psychic) ability, nor to dismiss the chance that in certain altered states of consciousness or perception a person might be able to detect information not normally accessible or apparent, but there is a very long way to go before such an approach can be thought of as a workable, reliable, research methodology in archaeology in any genuinely worthwhile sense. Nevertheless, to leave no stone unturned, so to speak, the DPT decided to attempt some preliminary experiments (mainly organised by DPT co-ordinator John Steele), by inviting a few self-proclaimed psychics on site at the Rollright complex at separate times to see if they could 'pick up' any information about the place from the past.

It proved problematic. For a start, dependably accurate psychics are very hard to find. Steele conducted double-blind tests using Mesolithic and Neolithic artefacts with a couple of psychics who were keen to work on the project. The results were worse than chance. Other psychics felt their sensitivities were too delicate to work at the Rollright site, and complained of headaches and sinister feelings when they got there. Yet others baulked at the idea of getting to the site in the early hours of the morning when much DPT work started at the site. (Sensitives, the DPT found, were sensitive in all sorts of ways!) Nevertheless, while we couldn't identify a psychic as apparently talented as Hamid or McMullen, a tiny handful of psychics were more approachable, and sessions were conducted. But results were still questionable. One psychic healer, for instance, went into trance at Rollright and saw entities within the ring of stones. He could describe these beings in detail. They told him that they possessed great knowledge, and would cease to exist if they left the circle of stones.

After cross-checking the results, it transpired that no psychic psychrometrised the same things at the same place. Thus, no coherent information – if actual information it was – managed to emerge from the sessions.

To many people, certainly academic scholars and archaeo-logical researchers, such experiments will be considered to be a waste of time. While I concur with that to a certain degree in general, in personal 'psychic readings' I've explored, definite, verifiable personal information was produced. What I typically observed was that during most of a session the sensitive, psychic, medium or whatever term you want to use, would bluff her way through, waffling on about dead uncle George on one occasion (I never had an uncle George), but, every so often, authentic information that she could definitely not have known about or inferred through normal channels would dart out like a fish from beneath a rock. It seems to me that authentic psychics need to produce a 'stream of consciousness' to carry the occasional flotsam of real information, but otherwise the running patter is likely to be chock full of their own beliefs, prejudices and guess-work. So, in my view, it is important on the one hand not to throw the baby out with the bathwater, but on the other not to

Figure 95. Psychics at work in the King's Men circle,
Rollright.

swallow everything that a psychic comes out with. That is why
in any future psychic archaeological research where tangible
evidence cannot be expected, at least the cross-referencing of
multiple independent and organised sessions at specific sites has
to be an essential aspect of methodology.

Sensory archaeology

While psychic archaeology remains anathema to mainstream
archaeological enquiry, the idea of sensory archaeology, the

conscious use of bodily senses in the study of ancient sites, landscapes and cultures, has quietly sidled into the discipline in the past few decades, and the interest in it has been increasing in recent years, as indicated by numerous books and academic papers tackling the topic from various angles (see, for just for examples, Hamilakis 2013; Day 2013; Butler and Purves 2013).

One, and possibly the main, sensory archaeological approach primarily focuses on ways of determining the nature of sensory conditions and experience in past societies through the study of tangible clues such as rock art, ancient paintings and carvings, pottery and other utensils or artefacts unearthed at ancient sites. Educated deduction, comparison to universal human sensory experience, flexible changes of perceptual habits by the investigator, and ethnological information where available, can sometimes be applied to the process. Another, 'looser' (academically speaking) approach is simply the direct sensory intake when visiting an ancient place, monument or landscape. This is often termed a 'phenomenological' approach – here's a definition of that term as given in the *Stanford Encyclopedia of Philosophy*:

> [P]henomenology is the study of "phenomena": appearances of things, or things as they appear in our experience, or *the ways we experience things* ... Phenomenology studies conscious experience as experienced from the subjective or first-person point of view. [My italics].

It is based on certain philosophical ideas that we won't go into here.

Naturally, we all experience places sensorially, phenomenologically, to some degree, but a serious sensory approach requires specific, conscious effort or awareness, which can be as simple as clapping your hands in an ancient sacred place or structure in order to see how and where the resultant echoes behave and originate in a monument or the surrounding environment (Devereux 2001). It can sometimes yield a greater understanding of the site's placement and even lead to new discoveries (for instance, see Bryn Celli Ddu in Part One).

Below are just a small handful of various examples of sensory archaeology, some of which involve mixed sensory modalities, though sound and sight are predominant. (We've already discussed the acoustic aspects of ancient places at some length in Part One, but following are a few cases which include sound in a specifically sensory archaeological context.)

SITE EXAMPLES

Places of puha

Researcher Chester Liwosz has been studying a narrow and deep ("slot") canyon in eastern California at the convergence zone of the Great Basin and the Mojave Desert. Not all rock art by any means is painted (pictograms) or incised petroglyphs: there is rock art within the canyon that has been *pecked*, usually with quartz hammerstones. Pecking images on rock surfaces causes sounds, and this has long been an appreciated acoustic aspect of rock art research. Ethnology of the area taught Liwosz that strong echoes and other sounds from rock surfaces were considered *puha*, locations that were the abode of spirits, holy places. He learned to 'read' the meaning of some of the various pecked motifs as relating to the kind of spirits inhabiting particular locations. He noted that much of the rock art was in places that were difficult or even dangerous to access, some with evidence of ancient toeholds. Getting up to the rock art sites, which were positioned at various levels and points along the canyon, required strenuous and sometimes risky climbing. Doing so, he appreciated that what was involved was a multi-sensory experience, involving sight, hearing, and touch:

> Climbing is a discursive practice, the body and space interact. Rock walls 'hear' and 'repeat' or 'respond' to the climbers' presence, while touching, holding, and enveloping them. For an animist, the canyon experiences the climbers, just as the latter does the former. At the culmination of their ascent, the climber here is faced or rewarded with an intense sensory experience of reinforcing sounds, vibrating air, intricate imagery, and an accomplished fatigue. Together, these components compose the synesthetic experience of a social interaction with a large and unique place. (Liwosz 2017)

Archaeologists Thomas Huffman and Frank Lee Earley, working in Colorado at the opposite, eastern, edge of the same Great Basin region to Liwosz, have traced an ancient Native American pilgrimage trail they found revealed in their interpretation of rock-art clues. The types of 'stations' along the route were varied, but many indicated places where it was believed *puha* was particularly strong. They add yet another sensory dimension: some of them consist of rocks which, when struck, produce sulphurous smells, which the authors suggest was "probably associated with *puha* emerging from the earth" – the veritable "smell of power" as they term it. (Huffman and Early 2019 op.cit)

In the Mountains of Dragons

Archaeologist and rock art expert, Aron Mazel, used literature detective work linked to his own field studies to unravel strands of evidence identifying the probable main sensory impetus that he reasons made the Didima (Ndedema) Gorge in the uKhahlamba region of the Drakensberg (Mountains of Dragons) in South Africa a rich rock art location containing some high-quality work. Indeed, with almost 4,000 paintings dating back up to 3,000 years in seventeen rock shelters, it is the richest concentration of San (Bushman) hunter-gatherer rock art in the whole country. It was clearly a major spiritual place for the ancient San. Mazel proposes that, "Didima Gorge's notable acoustic characteristics were central to the hunter-gatherer creation of its exceptional corpus of rock art" (Mazel 2011).

There would of course have been echoes and resonances from ritual activity – such as hand-clapping, foot stomping and use of ankle rattles – in the veritable echo chambers of rock shelters, but thunderstorm activity would seemingly be the primary acoustic agent at Didima. The legendary documenter of San/Bushman rock art in the Drakensberg, Harald Pager, who, along with his wife Shirley-Ann, spent years recording thousands of examples of rock shelter images in the Didima Gorge, remarked:

The name of the gorge is a Zulu one, meaning 'The Reverberating One', implying shaking and upheaval ... From our experience, it most likely applies to the commotion made during a thunderstorm, when each crash [of thunder] produces a clattering vibration as it echoes through the huge kranses [precipices] of the narrow gorge." (Pager et al. 1971)

It would not only be the audible sounds of the thunder, because thunder also contains low frequency components, even infra-sonics, which when not consciously heard can be *felt* vibrating within the body, sometimes producing eerie psychological sensations.

In personal communication with Mazel, Peter Raper, a linguist and expert in South African place-names, informed him that the name "didima/Ndedema" is actually of San origin, and refers to the echoing rumble of thunder during storms. According to Raper, an earlier variant of the name was 'Deduma': "The component *dum* of the early name ... is thought to be a Xhosa [Bantu language] adaptation of the /Xam [San language] word *!gum* to ... 'roar', bellow, call". (Note: the various pronunciation inserts relate to the fact these are what is known as 'click' languages.)

Mazel comments that it is likely "that Didima Gorge became an acoustic powerhouse, strongly resonant with spirits for the uKhahlamba-Drakensberg hunter-gatherers." This is further supported by researcher Riaan Rifkin:

> [It] is therefore conceivable that locations with marked acoustic characteristics were perceived as the dwelling places of spirits, and that such places were regarded as possessing vast amounts of supernatural potency. (Rifkin 2009)

It needs to be borne in mind that the San, like so many early peoples, conceived that rock surfaces and cliffs were in effect membranes behind which there was a spirit world (Part One), and so echoes, resonances and other sounds associated with rocks were freighted with spiritual significance.

Last word on sound and spirits in San tradition can go to a San bushman called /Han≠kass'o, as recorded by Bleek and Lloyd in 1878: "O beast of prey! Thou art the one who hearest the place behind, it is resonant with sound". This phrase is interpreted as referring to a powerful shaman (beast of prey) who is familiar with and visits the spirit world (the place behind). (Ouzman 2001)

Inca glitterati

Using a combination of literature, linguistic and field research, Australian scholar Ian Farrington studied the poorly researched site of Qespiwanka, an Inca (Inka) rural palace in Peru's Vilkanota Valley, northwest of Cuzco. He reveals that the *qespi* place-name element denotes qualities of brilliant light (shine, glitter, sparkle, in general), and the second element, *wanka* (*wank'a, wak'a*), denotes a shrine or sacred place. He explains that this place-name relates to the Inca King's role as 'Son of the Sun' (*Intip Churin*).

> Oracular consultation between the Sapa Inca and the sun was achieved when, during moments of qespi, the sun spoke bearing upon him legitimacy. Such authority was displayed in the clothing he wore, the objects he carried, the palaces in which he lived and the litter in which he travelled. Places, where communication took place, were revered and commemorated. (Farrington 2017)

Oracular consultation between the Sapa Inca (Quechua for the only, or great, Inca) and the sun was achieved when, during moments of *qespi*, the Sun 'spoke' conferring legitimacy on the king. The "moments of *qespi*" Farrington refers to seem to be a mystical trance or fugue state induced by a deep reverie while gazing at shiny material, such as quartz or gold, in which the king had his consultation with the Sun. (This might be likened to mystic trance in other religious traditions; one thinks of Jacob Boehme, for instance, a German mystic who was suddenly transported into a trance state while gazing at a pewter dish sparkling in the sunlight. He reckoned that in a quarter of an hour he saw and knew more than if he had been "many years together at a university".)

Farrington probed into Andean religio-cultural concepts about light, and notes that the Inca were part of a "pan-American aesthetic of brilliance" and a belief in the "spiritual and creative power of light" (Saunders 2003). Shininess was cosmologically charged, Farrington states. This could be the case with all kinds of shiny objects – crystals, metals, shells, even shiny wood, "as well as mica-tempered and burnished pottery", as well as reflected light from pools and mirrors. Such shiny, glittering, brilliant twinkles of light could act as 'portals' into other mental states/ spiritual realms, either spontaneously, or after meditation, seclusion, fasting or excessive ritual drinking of *aqha* (maize beer) or psychoactive *vilka* seeds or snuff.

Inca palace walls were clad in sheets of gold, and an Inca king would wear rich clothing such as a silver shirt, gold and silver bracelets, gold pectorals and bejeweled necklaces, and garment attachments such as mirrors. He would be "wearing light" as Saunders has put it. When the last Inca king, Atawallpa (Atahualpa), met the Spanish invaders, Pizarro said he "was wearing so much gold and silver, that it shone brightly in the sun".

This linguistic research enabled Farrington to explicate the nature of Qespiwanka's features.

At Qespiwanka, the *wank'a* itself is a large boulder of whitish crystalline granite, that is situated more or less in the geographical centre of the plaza … It stands up to 2.43m in height, about 5.5m in length, 3.6m wide and probably weighs in the order of 30 metric tons. It has a distinctive form, dominated by a rounded dome in its northeastern centre, a characteristic of other important rocks elsewhere in the Cusco heartland, an upper sloping surface that tapers down towards the southwest, and a lower, almost vertical face, extending 0.6-1m above the ground...

...While the Quespiwanka rock is not on a platform, and it is neither small, artificially erected nor an outcrop, it can be considered to have been part of a *usnu* complex [an official observation and ceremonial platform], because of its location and because it has two vital cosmological components, its height as well as a canal to receive and remove any offerings. The rock itself has not been carved but in many places, particularly on its top and upper eastern, northern and northwestern sides, its surface has been altered by being repeatedly pounded with stone hammers. This has removed much of its boulder patina to reveal a crisp, bright white crystalline surface, that would have flashed as it was worked and even today it glitters in the sun. In other words, the rock has been deliberately modified to display *qespi*; its animated crystal surface twinkling throughout the day as sunlight fell upon it, enhancing its role as the focal point of the palace plaza and perhaps as a place where consultation with the sun could occur. (Farrington op cit.)

And there is more. On the skylines around the site are four Inca-constructed towers, marking sightlines which from the Qespiwanka rock indicate the sun rise and set points at the June and December solstices. All in all, a fitting place for the Son of the Sun to consult his god.

Double sunrise at Avebury

I personally conducted a case of phenomenologically-based sensory archaeology a few decades ago at the Avebury complex in Wiltshire, England. This lies 32km (20 miles) north of Stonehenge, and comprises a great henge monument much larger than Stonehenge, consisting of a roughly circular bank-and-ditch earthwork enclosing more than 11ha (28 acres) containing a great ring of standing stones which has further stone settings within its circumference.

In the Neolithic landscape surrounding the henge is the West Kennet Avenue of standing stones running southwards, barely visible remnants of Beckhampton Avenue running westwards from the henge, and a multi-ringed feature known as the Sanctuary at the far end of the West Kennet Avenue, plus linear burial mounds like East Kennet and West Kennet Long

Figure 96. Part of the south-west quadrant of great stone circle and henge
(ditch and bank) of Avebury, Wiltshire, England.

Barrows. Silbury Hill (c.2,500 B.C.) stands like a hub approximately in the middle of the whole complex – it is Europe's tallest artificial prehistoric mound, built upon a small existing natural mound. It was also constructed in an unusual manner in the Neolithic world: tiered rings of chalk walls filled with debris then covered over with earth. It created a remarkably stable structure preserving the profile of the monument over thousands of years.

The final shape of the mound looks a little like a gigantic plum pudding. It has a flat summit about 40m (130 feet) above ground, with smooth, even sides, except for an eroded ledge running around about 5m below the summit. (This is the remnant of one of the construction tiers that was re-cut in Roman times.) The mound has been excavated a number of times but no burial or central chamber has ever been discovered. Rather, a set of possibly symbolic sarsen stones were found inside. (An 18th-century excavation of a narrow deep cavity with oak fragments at its base have led to ideas that there may originally have been a 'totem pole' in the heart of Silbury.) Excavators also found grasses that were remarkably well-preserved – still green, after nearly 5,000 years. They held the remnants of flying ants, indicating that the building of Silbury had started one long-ago summer around the end of July or early in August – Lammas in the Christian calendar, Lughnasa in the pagan Celtic one. Harvest time.

Now, I had visited the Avebury complex in all seasons over many years, thinking that because here we have a relatively well-preserved Neolithic landscape, I should be able to make sense of it – to 'decode' it, so to say. But I couldn't – that is until I had a flash of insight in a dramatic phenomenological manner, I needn't go into full detail here (but I have elsewhere – see Devereux 1992). As a consequence, by detailed scrutiny of the Avebury landscape and its monuments I finally began to *see* it.

From whichever of the older encircling monuments Silbury Hill is viewed, it is so positioned that the skyline behind it always appears to intersect its profile at the level of the summit-to-ledge segment of the great mound. And when viewed from the point where the tallest stone once stood within the henge, this top segment appears visually wedged between the distant horizon and the intervening slope of a natural ridge called Waden Hill. But just before harvesting, around the time of year when Silbury began to be built, cereal crops being grown on the Waden ridge (in Neolithic times as now) obscure this sightline.

Silbury was therefore tightly positioned within the contours of the natural topography. But why was such a majestic mound built immediately alongside Waden Hill, which is virtually the same height as itself (see Figure 15)? I eventually discovered that

Figure 97. Silbury Hill viewed from the western end of West Kennet Long Barrow (an early Neolithic structure but which has a later Neolithic extension to the west that enables this sightline). The far skyline that can be seen intersecting the mound's profile is formed by Windmill Hill, which was being used as a prehistoric ceremonial gathering place long before any of the Avebury monuments were built. It may possibly have been viewed as an ancestral place by the Stone Age builders of the Avebury complex.

Figure 98. At equinoctial periods of the year an observer on the summit of
Silbury Hill sees a 'double sunrise': (a) first over the distant horizon then (b)
a few minutes later, by moving down to the ledge in the slope 5m (17ft) below,
again over the near skyline formed by adjacent Waden Hill.

in late July/early August, and in early May (Beltane in the pagan
Celtic tradition), when the sun rises along the same segment
of the eastern horizon, an observer on top of Silbury sees the
sunrise burst over the distance skyline and then, by going down
to the ledge, it can be seen as if rising a second time a few minutes
later over the ridge-back of close-by Waden Hill. Silbury is thus
built to exactly the right height, in precisely the right place, to
visually separate the near and far eastern horizons, allowing
a celebratory 'double sunrise' at two key times of the ancient
ceremonial and agricultural year (Devereux 1991, 1992, op.cit.,
2010 op.cit.; Barrett 1994).

Figure 99. The 'glory' optical effect seen glowing at the tip of Silbury's shadow as viewed from the monument's summit. With the naked eye it can be faintly detected reaching to the western skyline.

There is an additional theatrical effect: a striking golden glow radiates westwards from the tip of Silbury's long shadow thrown by the rising sun. This is a 'glory' or 'Brocken Spectre' – an optical phenomenon created by the myriad prisms formed by dew drops on the grass and crop fields to the west of the mound. During this remarkable event, when one is present on top of Silbury (no longer permitted due to damage being caused to the monument), it feels as if the great mound is casting a blessing across the land. Seen in this way, Silbury is a harvest hill and perhaps was even perceived by Neolithic eyes as the representation of the bountiful Earth Mother goddess. I felt privileged and deeply moved to notice something that had not been recorded for five millennia.

Stone Age cameras

A pioneering new strand of sensory archaeology has been emerging in recent times called 'archaeo-optics'. There are two, very different, basic types of this: a highly technical one that includes, for example, such techniques as 3D laser scanning in which virtually invisible rock engravings are scanned to better reveal them or 3D photogrammetry methods that can produce 3D digital models of features such as standing stones, and the other is by contrast phenomenological. This approach essentially relates to optical effects observed and recorded in situ at monumental sites by careful and close observation (the 'glory' at Silbury Hill, above, is one example of this).

An especially exciting archaeological development of this latter type is currently being pursued by a small number of pioneers. It mainly revolves around the 'Camera Obscura' (Latin for 'dark room') or pinhole camera effect, in which light entering a dark space through a very small aperture can project an inverted and reversed image of the exterior onto the rear surface of the dark space. It is the creation of an illuminated image without means of a lens. (A simple version of this can be seen if one pulls heavy curtains almost closed leaving just a tiny chink between them – if it is a bright day outside, a moving coloured image of scudding clouds, people or traffic will be projected onto the opposite wall of the darkened room.) The effect was being used by artists as far back as the 16th Century, and maybe long before.

This effect can occur in various types of archaeological site containing an enclosed chamber where light can reach it through a narrow, restricted aperture, but particularly ideal types of site for studying this kind of effect are megalithic passage tombs, which essentially consist of a narrow passage with a small opening leading into a dark chamber – the basic architecture of a camera obscura.

I was first made aware of the optical potential of passage tombs in the late 1970s, by a report of effects at the Orkney, Scotland, site of Maeshowe (c.2,750 B.C.): writing in *The*

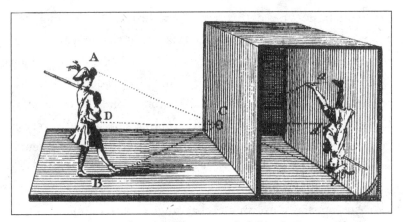

Figure 100. An 18th-century depiction of a full-scale Camera Obscura

Ley Hunter (TLH 73, 1976), artist Chris Castle reported on his suspicion that there could be a camera obscura effect at Maeshowe after he noticed some anomalies on photographs he had taken from inside the monument, looking out through the entrance passage (which aligns to a sunset around midwinter and to a monolith, the Barnhouse Stone, a fairly short distance away). And there was further discussion about this possibility a year later by photographer Colin Bord in TLH 75.

But there the matter lay dormant for many years. But now, interest in the camera obscura effect is being revived. A leading researcher in this field is archaeologist and artist Aaron Watson. He and various colleagues have been conducting serious archaeo-optical research at a range of passage grave monuments. He writes on his website:

Archaeo-optic phenomena are especially effective at passage graves because they reproduce the fundamental format of a camera obscura. The restricted single entrances govern the movement of light to such an extent that only

Figure 101. Examples of the entrance passages leading into central chambers inside Neolithic passage tombs. (a) Looking out along the entrance passage of Maeshowe, Orkney [Photo: Rob Burke/Wikimedia Commons/CC BY-SA 2.00] (b) Looking out along the entrance passage to Bryn Celli Ddu, Anglesey, Wales. (c) Looking inwards down one of the two passages into Knowth, the larger companion to Newgrange, Ireland. (d) Looking inwards down the entrance passage at Gavrinis, France.

simple refinements are needed to manifest a visible image. Some sites even have original built-in features that may have served this purpose. At others the effect can be achieved by using an opaque screen punctured with a small hole ... the dark chambers of these monuments provide the perfect venue within which optical projections can be witnessed, but their extended passages allow the size, brightness and focus of projections to be closely controlled. (Watson, http://www.aaronwatson.co.uk/archaeooptics-overview)

The "opaque screen" Watson refers to is an animal hide with a small perforation draped over the passage entrance. Stone Age technology. He has created projected images inside a wide range of monuments, such as Bryn Celli Ddu in Wales, Carrowkeel Cairn G, County Sligo, Ireland, and a number of sites in Orkney, including the Tomb of the Eagles (Isbister) and the Dwarfie Stane, which we described previously. Watson's main collaborator has been Ronnie Scott, himself an archaeologist and artist (Watson and Scott 2017). Other helpers over the years have included Kieran Baxter, Diane O'Leary and Alice Watterson.

Another important researcher in this pioneering field is Mike Gatton, who also has explored projected images inside passage graves and who did, in fact, advise and encourage Watson in his work. He says on his website (http://paleo-camera.com/) that he specializes "in the aesthetic and ritual use of light in prehistory and antiquity, with particular emphasis on the phenomenon of the camera obscura, an optical principle as old as light itself".

Gatton isn't tied specifically to Neolithic structures – an especially interesting case that came under his consideration concerned the ancient Greek 'Mystery Temple' of Eleusis, west of Athens. The mysteries were enacted here annually in September.

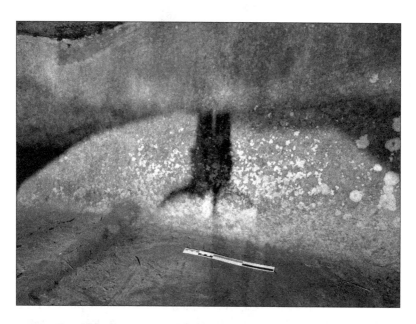

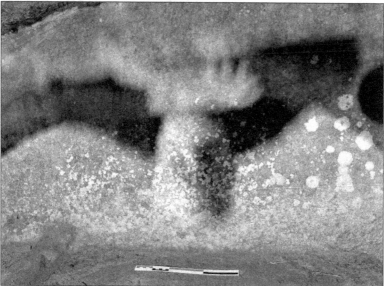

Figure 102. Enhanced digital photos showing optical inverted projections of a human figure upon the chamber wall of the Dwarfie Stane, Orkney. [Photos: Aaron Watson]

The *mystai* (initiatory candidates) were led through a day-long set of rituals, possibly imbibing a psychoactive drink based on ergot, a parasite of rye. Finally, they assembled in the Telesterion, a vast building unlike other Greek temple architecture in that it had a plain, undecorated exterior. Inside, there was a forest of columns and an inner enclosure known as the Anaktoron. Although the Telesterion had been rebuilt and enlarged numerous times, the central structure remained unaltered. In the great, final revelation of the mysteries, the *epopteia*, flames erupted from the only doorway in the Anaktoron and there was a manifestation of the goddess Persephone. The nature of this mystery was kept a secret on pain of death or exile, but those who experienced it – and this included many notable names of Classical Greece – felt their lives to have been changed. Gatton has proposed an archaeo-optical explanation of the *epopteia*. In the abstract of his paper detailing the proposed solution, he writes:

> How was the apparition of the goddess conjured? This study surveys extant epigraphical and archaeological information to formulate a research question: could the Anaktoron have acted as a box of light, a fire illuminating figurines and projecting their images out into the darkened Telesterion? A set of experiments was performed that confirmed the operational feasibility of an 'Eleusinian Projector'. The appearance of the goddess as light can be explained physically as well as mythologically. (Gatton 2017)

The sensory approach can have many other archaeo-optic aspects, such as observing and recording the play of sunlight, moonlight or shadows inside monuments or across ancient features. To take just one example, the light play in Cairn T, a chambered and carved cairn on top of one of the Loughcrew Hills in Ireland. Here, the

Figure 103. Remnants of part of the Telesterion at the Mystery Temple of Eleusis – even the columns have been reduced to mere stumps.

rising equinoctial sun reaches into the chamber with a dazzling golden light. The shape and angle of the entrance passage causes the sunlight to cast a fairly regular rectangular patch on the inner walls of the passage and chamber, inching across the images carved there (Brennan 1983). On its journey into and out of the mound the shape of the sunlight crosses and frames a sequence of rock carvings. On the day of the equinox, the rectangle of sunlight reaches its furthest point into the chamber, framing a rayed carving on the rear stone (Figure 104). This carving has eight 'rays' or 'petals', presumably a symbolic representation of the archaic eight divisions of the solar year (two solstices, two equinoxes, and four 'cross-quarter' days), and even of the sun itself. The ceremonialists of the Stone Age were nothing if not showmen.

* * * * *

All in all, as sensory archaeology continues to grow, especially as it currently is doing to a large extent through the sensibilities

Figure 104. A rubbing of the eight-'rayed' (or 'petalled')
rock art image in Cairn T, Loughcrew, Ireland.

of archaeologically-informed artists, it will open up many more insights regarding a whole host of ancient places around the world. Linked to archaeoacoustics and archaeoastronomy where relevant, this sensory approach can make them come alive, allowing us to briefly glimpse as if through ancient eyes and hear as if through ancient ears.

6

DREAMTIME

I had a particularly vivid dream – in 1990 in Manhattan, curiously enough – about the Dragon Project, I suppose unsurprisingly as it was occupying much of my thinking at the time. In the dream people were sleeping at ancient sites. So, it was a dream about dreaming. This prompted me to suggest that the DPT take on a planned programme of dreaming at selected ancient sites, to test the remote possibility that the dreaming mind might sense things, pick up things, that the waking mind might not or might miss. A kind of whole extra dimension to primary sensing.

It sounded crazy, and turned out to be something akin to a nightmare in a logistical sense, but the idea didn't come out of a vacuum: for me, there were a few reasons, apart from my dream. One was that from literature research I knew there had been serious work on apparent so-called paranormal activity in dreams (Krippner et al. 1973), and also reports on interactions between dreaming and objective verification. A fine example of this was given by anthropologist Marianne George concerning her field-work with the Barok people of New Ireland, Papua New Guinea.

GRIMAN

George experienced extraordinary instances of transpersonal dreaming with the Barok. The community's 'big woman' (chief),

234   The Powers of Ancient and Sacred Places

Kalerian, sent the anthropologist messages while she was asleep. George didn't realise this was happening at first until two of Kalerian's sons, Alek and Bustaman, visited her early one morning.

"Did you understand what our mother was telling you?" they enquired.

George was nonplussed. "Who?"

"My mother was talking to you last night," Alek answered, watching the anthropologist closely.

"I did not talk to her last night," a confused George replied.

"Do you not remember? When she came to see you in the night?" Alek persisted. "In Tokpisin we call this *griman* – dreaming."

George then recalled that she did indeed have a dream the previous night in which Kalerian directed her to do something about a problem. The anthropologist told the sons that she couldn't remember much about what Kalerian had said to her in the dream. They explained that was why she had sent them round, and repeated the exact words their mother had said in the dream. With a deep ontological shock, George realised these boys had been informed by their mother what she had dreamt the night before.

"Do you always do this, communicate with people – visit people – in their dreams at night?" George wanted to know. The sons indicated it was what "big people" could do, and that it could happen over long distances as well as within the village. George started to make more of an effort to remember her dreams.

By the time George arrived in the village for her next anthropological visit to the Barok, Kalerian had died. But soon after her arrival, the anthropologist had a dream featuring the dead Kalerian. This time, George had a clear recall of it when she awoke. When she met Alek that day she asked if he had seen his mother in a dream. Alek said no, but wanted to know if anyone else had been in the dream. There had been, one of Alek's brothers, Tadi, who was now a "big man" in another village. George was advised to visit Tadi and tell him about the dream.

"So, she is talking with you," Tadi observed. He confided that his mother had passed the gift of *griman* on to him, and it was that power which made him a big man. "She visits you in dreams," Tadi informed George. "I am telling you so you can understand this."

During her third visit to New Ireland, in 1985, George wanted to find the foundations of an ancient clan house, a type of ritual building typically found in Barok villages. This ancient example had been high up the mountainside but George was unable to find the exact location where it had once stood. Then one night she had a dream in which she and Kalerian were at the site of the old clan house, and while speaking intently, the dead woman pointed to the roots of a tree that had overgrown one end of the area. The next morning, Alek joined the anthropologist for breakfast tea.

"Did you understand where she showed you to look?" he asked in his typically direct way.

"Oh, you mean what Kalerian was telling me in my dream?" George stuttered, this time a little better prepared. "Yes, I saw her, but I didn't really understand what she meant."

"You want to find the old hearth of that clan house, right?"

"Yes!"

Alek went on to describe in detail the roots of the tree George had seen in her dream. George realised he could not have known those details except from her dream.

Later that day, George and a visiting European researcher went up to the site. She told her companion about the dream, but he didn't take it seriously. They found the tree but the European insisted that they dig on both sides of it and not just the spot that had been indicated in George's dream. They first dug on the opposite side of the tree to the one George wanted to test, and found nothing. So George started digging among the roots where Kalerian had pointed in the dream. It was hard going but they eventually found some charcoal that the two excavators were able to bag for dating – the hearth was exactly where the deceased Kalerian had indicated in the dream.

The phenomenon of *griman* is remarkable enough, let alone apparent discarnate messaging within it, so it is with good reason that George comments: "I wrote about what happened in my journal – in code, just in case anything happened to me. I did not want anyone to end up reading about it and thinking that I had gone nuts in the field." (George 1995)

SACRED AND HEALING DREAMING

Another important reason that lay behind the idea for the DPT dreamwork programme was because there were already long and established traditions in the ancient world of sleeping at sacred sites, usually referred to as 'temple sleep', as discussed in previous chapters. This, as we noted, involved sleeping at a special temple or a venerated natural site with the aim of having dreams for initiation, divination or healing purposes. Certain ritual actions known as 'incubation' would be conducted prior to sleep to help direct the dreamer's mind.

Such dream-seeking procedures go back to the dawn of history. Jewish seers in antiquity would resort to a grave or sepulchral vault and spend the night there in order that the spirit of the deceased would appear in a dream and offer information or guidance. Indeed, the Jews were considered to be potent dream interpreters by the Babylonians, and this is encapsulated in the Biblical story of Daniel who was called on to interpret the dreams of King Nebuchadnezzar. Dynastic Egypt had special temples for incubatory rituals where supplicants would fast and recite specific prayers. Immediately before going to sleep, the dream candidate might also invoke the help of suitable deities by writing their names on a piece of clean linen, then burning it. A classic example of an ancient Egyptian divinatory dream is that of the pharaoh, Thutmose IV (c.1419 – 1386 B.C.). Before Thutmose ascended to the kingship of Egypt the god Hormakhu appeared to him in a dream, foretelling of riches and a united kingdom when he came to power. This all came to pass, and the pharaoh recorded the dream on a stela (stone pillar) that still stands before the Sphinx to this day. China, too, had incubation temples, and they were active up until the 16th Century. The incubated dreams were used mainly as aids to political decision-making and state officials would spend a night at such a temple before important meetings. In Japan, the emperor had a dream hall in his palace where he would sleep on a polished stone bed called a *kamudoko* when he wanted help in resolving a matter of state.

And, of course, as already discussed in Chapter 3, sacred sleeping was widely practiced in ancient Greece. It was known as *psychomanteia* and was primarily aimed at finding cures for disease. It accompanied the rise in popularity of the healing god, Asclepius, son of Apollo. Over three hundred dream temples dedicated to the god were built throughout Greece and the eastern Mediterranean area. The first such Asclepeion was in Athens, but the most important was at Epidaurus. Temple assistants known as *therapeutes* (presumably where we get our term 'therapy' from) would later interpret supplicants' dreams for them, advising on the course of treatment indicated by the dream imagery. (There is evidence that the floors of *abatons* were sometimes covered in blood, suggesting that actual surgery may have been performed.)

The Romans adopted and adapted the idea of dream temples, so it is not surprising that they have been found throughout the Roman Empire. One of the most far-flung was the Temple of Nodens, located over a powerful spring in Lydney Park, Gloucestershire, and overlooking the River Severn. Nodens was a native British god, patron of hunting and healing and who also had water associations. The sacred animals of this precinct were dogs, judging by the number of votive canine figurines that have been unearthed there. Like the snakes of Asclepius, they would have been used to lick patients' afflicted parts.

Healing sleep in some Christian churches was also practiced in the Middle Ages, and temple sleep continues in some countries to this day. This is exemplified by the Shiva shrine at Tarakeswar, north of Calcutta in India. Pilgrims suffering chronic or incurable diseases undertake dream incubation at the site, a procedure known as *dharna* in Bengali. Under the guidance of a priest, the sick person fasts for a period then sleeps in a specified area within the temple.

Haunted by dreams

There is a curious modern footnote to the ancient Greek temple sleep tradition. The novelist and poet, the late Lawrence Durrell, made some astounding if now long-forgotten observations (in *The Listener*, 25 September, 1947). On his first visit to Epidaurus in 1939, his sense was that the whole area held an aura of sanctity – there was "something at once intimate and healing about it". But his Greek guide at the complex let it slip that he had managed to finagle a transfer to Mycenae. Durrell wanted to know why the man should want to leave this peaceful place in favour of the craggy citadel. "I can't bear the dreams we have in this valley," the guide explained. "What dreams?" Durrell queried. "Everybody in this valley has dreams," the man replied. "Some people don't mind, but as for me, I'm off." He went on to comment that the dreams frequently contained the figure of a man with an Assyrian-looking visage, with dense ringlets falling down onto his shoulders. He looked like a figure depicted in an ancient fresco in the Epidaurus museum. Surely that was to be expected, considering that the guide spent his days in Epidaurus, Durrell suggested to the guide. "Why should my two kids dream about him when they have never set foot in the museum?" the Greek retorted. "If you don't believe me, ask any of the peasants who live in this valley. They all have dreams. The valley is full of dreams." Durrell began to wonder if the thousands of dreams countless supplicants had experienced at Epidaurus over its centuries of activity had somehow lingered on.

In 1945, immediately after the Second World War, Durrell had reason to revisit this train of thought. While visiting the Greek island of Kos, he encountered two British soldiers who were clearing up scattered German and Italian ordnance; they were camped near the great Asclepeion there (Chapter 3). Durrell chatted with the soldiers who asked him if he knew anything about the temple. He told them about the Asclepius cult, and casually asked them if they had noticed anything unusual about their dreams. This startled them. It transpired that they had moved their tent out of their initial camping spot within the temple precinct precisely because they had experienced profoundly odd and disturbing dreams.

"Was it possible, I found myself wondering again, that dreams do not disappear?" Durrell wrote. "And especially in a place like this which must have been charged with hundreds of thousands of dreams?"

But dreams are supposed to live only inside one's head, surely? If some current theorists are correct, perhaps not. They argue that mind is a *field* rather than some kind of buzz produced by brain activity, that our neurons process a raw 'mind-stuff' inherent in the fabric of the universe and create what we call human consciousness. Biologist Rupert Sheldrake, perhaps the most well-known proponent of the mind-as-a-field view rather than mind, consciousness, being the sole product of complex interactions in the brain, has proposed a controversial theory he calls *morphic resonance*. His theory states that a person, or any individual organism, is informed by a memory field belonging to the species as a whole. (Sheldrake 1981)

Could memory fields also attach to *places*? Could the dreaming mind be able to access a site's information at this subtle level? And if the place was once felt to be sacred might it hold more 'memory field' imprints than a secular one due to intense spiritual and purposeful usage? Durrell decided to conduct his own experiment by sleeping in the Kos temple, and recording his dreams in a notebook. Unfortunately, it seems he did not publish these because he felt the experiment was not complete.

So, over half a century later, encouraged by a dream in Manhattan, the DPT decided to conduct a similar but more extended experiment.

THE ANCIENT SITES DREAMWORK PROGRAMME

The basic plan for the programme was to run as many dream sessions as possible at just four selected ancient sites, each of them possessing some form of geophysical anomaly. The sleep volunteers were to be drawn from a wide range of people, each volunteer to be accompanied by at least one helper to watch for a rocking and rolling action beneath the volunteer sleeper's closed eyelids (Rapid

Eye Movements or R.E.M), which denotes dreaming sleep. At these points the sleeper was to be awoken and a report of any dreams at that time audio-recorded in situ, directly from the dreamer, and later transcribed. The programme was aimed at making on-site dreaming as transpersonal and objective as possible: on-site dreamers were to hold their sessions separately to others. An original main aim was to see if there arose elements in the dreams – scenes, themes, sequences, images, motifs, symbols, even colours – that were *site specific*.

Figure 105. Professor Stanley Krippner, consultant to the DPT's dreamwork programme. He visited the four sites, and studied the final output of transcribed dreams, producing academic papers on the material.

Dr. Stanley Krippner, a renowned American expert in dream analysis, and highly informed on aspects of parapsychological research, was invited to be the programme's consultant, and he kindly agreed.

The sites

All four sites that were chosen for the programme contained a magnetic or radiation anomaly. Three of them were prehistoric monuments, all located in the Land's End district of Cornwall, the other one was a natural site. Here are the four.

Chûn Quoit

Figure 106. Chûn Quoit dolmen, Land's End, Cornwall.

Chûn Quoit is a Neolithic granite dolmen dating to c.3,000 B.C. or earlier, standing isolated on high moorland near the north Cornish coast. Because of the granite, its interior produces a higher than background radiation count (about the same as the interior of the King's Chamber in Egypt's Great Pyramid, in fact.)

Madron Well

This holy well is located in the ruins of a tiny medieval chapel standing in woodland. The actual spring is close by and water is

Figure 107. The font-like well in Madron chapel.

transferred from there to a granite, font-like well in the corner
of the now roofless chapel through granite conduits. Due to the
granitic stone, the water has a higher than background radiation
count. Up until about the 19th Century, some local 'wise woman'
(the last one recorded was An' [Aunt] Katty) would attend the
actual spring, which according to a 1910 photograph, was once
surrounded by massive blocks of granite.

Appropriately enough, an ancient healing ritual involving sleep
was carried out at this place up until recent centuries. This was such
a powerful pagan tradition that local Christianity did not attempt
to ban it but 'Christianised' it instead by building the little chapel.
The healing procedure we have records of occurred in this Christianised setting inside the chapel. Sick children were brought to the
waters, stripped naked, plunged three times into it. Then, the child
would be clothed, wrapped in a blanket and made to sleep nearby
while a strip of their clothing (a 'clootie', or 'jowd' in Cornish) was
hung on a nearby hawthorn tree – the magical rationale being the
child's condition would improve as the fabric rotted.

In the early 17th Century, John Thomas and William Cork,
both crippled, were cured enough for one to resume work as a
fisherman and the other to serve in the army: they had made

three annual visits to the well on a specific date to effect their cures. A particularly famous healing was that of John Trelil, who had been paralysed from the waist down since having a child-hood accident. He was helped to the chapel well on the first three Thursdays in May, each time bathing in the waters and then sleeping on an artificial mound called 'St Madern's Bed' beside the chapel's altar slab. Four years later he was fit enough to enlist in the army. This seemingly miraculous cure was recorded by Bishop Hall of Exeter in his "Treatise on the Invisible World" in 1640. (Weatherhill and Devereux 1994)

It was my own experience at Madron that helped to confirm its inclusion in the DPT's list of selected dreamwork programme sites. I visited the ruined chapel alone one balmy summer after-noon. It was such a soporific atmosphere that I lay down on a ledge running along one side of the chapel listening to the spring water tinkling into the font/well and soon fell asleep. A vivid dream awoke me after about ten minutes: two disembodied female hands floated in front of me and dipped themselves in the well waters, then applied their moist fingers around my dream eyes in a specific way. (I know this sounds too good to be true, but it is, nevertheless, true.) I immediately arose, went to the corner well and performed the exact same procedure on myself.

Carn Ingli

This already-discussed place is the one natural location of the four selected sites. People resorted to it from at least as far back as c.5,000 B.C. for purposes unknown. By the 6th Century A.D., it was used periodically for prayer and fasting by St. Brynach, an anchorite who had his cell in the nearby hamlet of Nevern.

Figure 108. The craggy summit of Carn Ingli, Preseli
Hills, South Wales. A magnetic anomaly spot.

Carn Euny

This is an underground passage with an attached circular, formerly corbelled, side-chamber situated beneath an Iron Age village,
so is dated to late centuries B.C. It is constructed with granite
stones, and thus its interior has higher than background radioactivity. In Cornwall, sites like these are called *fogous*, the Cornish
term for subterranean stone-lined passageways or galleries which
are typically termed *souterrains* where they occur elsewhere –
Ireland, Brittany, north-east Scotland, and the Orkney islands.

There has been stiff debate about their function. The orthodox view has been that they were refuges in times of trouble or,
the more popular idea, that they were storage places. An alternative view, however, is that they were intended for ritual or
ceremonial purposes. There is no direct, clear evidence for any of
these views, and it may also be an error to assume all such underground structures as these were intended for the same function
in the different regions in which they occur. The side-chamber in
this case possibly suggests some ritual use.

Figure 109. Inside the Carn Euny fogou. The circular
corbelled chamber leads off to the left in this view.

General procedure

The volunteer dreamers who became involved in the exercise came
from many walks of life and various countries, ranging in age from
teenagers to senior citizens, though most were in their thirties
and forties. They were asked to record six dreams obtained in
their familiar home environment for comparison with any on-site
dreams they had. A local DPT facilitator then took them to the site
they had selected from the four sites designated by the DPT. The
dream volunteers would snuggle into a sleeping bag and, usually,
fall asleep a little before midnight. Using a shaded or red-filtered
flashlight, a helper checked periodically for REMs. Dreamers were
awoken when these occurred and had their dream reports immediately tape-recorded. These were later transcribed.

The transcripts were then sent to Krippner in San Francisco.
There they were re-typed onto standardised forms so work could
commence on processing their data; this involved tabulating the
dream elements according to professionally accepted dream
analytical tools.

For the purposes of future and ongoing research, the transcripts have finally been digitised to allow for faster professional searches. Unfortunately, this will happen months or even years after publication of the present book, but some preliminary probing of the on-site dreaming content is to be included here.

Preliminary results

It took until the year 2000, the close of the fieldwork part of the DPT's Ancient Sites Dreamwork Programme, to assemble any sort of compilation of dream content data allowing for some level of study. This may seem surprising to anyone not familiar with the problems and difficulties and limits of such ambitious but unfunded research efforts. It was a learning experience for the DPT, and nobody else was making such an organised attempt.

The initial problems soon became apparent: the enthusiasm of many people who were enticed with the romanticism of the idea of dreaming at very ancient sites tended to pale as they were faced with the hard reality of what was required. Even some of those who eventually got into the field with DPT facilitators became nervous when they arrived at a remote site on wild moorland in the dead of night amidst driving rain or howling wind, as was sometimes the case. We glimpsed more than a few facial expressions of "I wish I hadn't agreed to this," from some of them!

Then there was a further problem in that all volunteers were asked for home (control) dreams before they did their on-site dreaming to allow for a statistical comparison to be made, but far too many failed to provide this – a procedural failure on the DPT's part, really, for not being strong enough to insist, but when a session had been arranged with some difficulty and the volunteer arrived saying they would do the home dream record later, it was something of a *fait accompli*. The upshot was that there was too little of the dream content material obtained at the sites that was adequate for any truly statistically significant study to be made. Nevertheless, what existed of the on-site dream content material that had been paired with home control dream material was passed to two judges, working blind and independently, and using accepted, professional evaluation measures. Two or three academic papers were produced. The first to be published was "The Use of the Strauch Scale to Study Dream Reports from Sacred Sites in England and Wales" in 2003 (Krippner et al. 2003). The abstract read:

Thirty-five volunteers spent between one and five nights in one of four unfamiliar outdoor "sacred sites" in England and Wales where they were awakened following rapid eye movement periods and asked for dream recall. They also monitored their dreams in familiar home surroundings, keeping dream diaries. Equal numbers of site dreams and home dream reports were obtained for each volunteer. Two judges, working blind and independently, evaluated each of the resulting 206 dream reports, using the Strauch Scale which contains criteria for identifying "bizarre," "magical," and "paranormal" elements. Of the 103 site dream reports, 46 fell into one of these categories, versus 31 of the home dream reports. A number of explanations exist for this difference, including expectancy, suggestion, the effect of unfamiliar surroundings, the nature of the volunteers' awakenings, and possible anomalous properties of the sacred sites. The latter possibility, however, is unlikely due to the fact the 22 volunteers reported site dreams containing Strauch Scale items, while 20 reported home dreams containing these content items, a minimal difference.

There simply wasn't the necessary body of workable material to conduct a fully-fledged statistical analysis.

In the same year, *Fortean Times* carried an article on the DPT ancient sites dreamwork programme as its cover story (*Fortean Times* 178, December).

In 2007, another academic paper was published, using the same on-site dream content raw material as in 2003, but this time using a different analytic tool, the Hall-Van de Castle Scale (Krippner et al. 2007). Part of the abstract reads:

> The 204 dream reports had previously been subjected to inspection for bizarre and paranormal content, with no significant differences. This analysis used the Hall-Van de Castle Scale, and several differences were found, most notably more aggressive content in site dreams and more friendly content in home dreams. In addition, home dream reports contained more incidences of failure, striving, and success. A number of explanations were proposed for these differences, including expectancy, suggestion, the effect of unfamiliar surroundings, and possible anomalous properties of the sacred sites.

Later in the paper it points out the rare nature of the DPT's ancient sites dream content material as a recorded body of research; with or without the comprehensive site-home dream comparisons it provides a "much needed addition to previous research that has focused on dream content influenced by the built environment." Although everyone on the DPT recognised the shortcomings of what had been, after all, a somewhat amateur, pioneer study, it was felt that whatever data it yielded would not have existed previously, and could be fed into entirely other, unrelated dream research. In fact, by 2006 this had already started to happen, as evidenced by an academic paper entitled "Cognitive Differences in Dream Content between English Males and Females Attending Dream Seminars Using Quantitative Content Analysis", in which some of the DPT's on-site dream material was involved (Tartz et al. 2006).

With place in mind

The original main aim of the dream programme, however, was to look for *site-specific* dream content material occurring in different volunteer's dreams – *transpersonal* dream imagery with the only connection being the site. In effect, to use the four sites as controls between themselves. As already noted, to see if any scenes, themes, images, motifs, symbols, even colours recurred at any one of the sites in contrast to the others, and also if any specific transpersonal content in dreams occurred. So, for the purposes of this book, we can take a little foray into some of the now digitised dream content material – though a proper, full computerised exploration of all the variables has yet to be started. In any case, much more on-site dream material would need to be collected and added to what exists for there to be any kind of an in-depth site-specific study. But I was keen to see if there were any faint hints in what we did have in what was, after all, just a pilot experiment.

In the brief examples presented below, the dream recalls are identified with the volunteer's initials. (Each of the dreamers was recorded separately, and remember that there was no cross-communication and most never even met one another.) And note that the dream contents are given in a rather disjointed and episodic manner – characteristic of them being reported verbally directly on awakening from REM sleep, rather than at a later point when memory tends to 'smooth' a dream's narrative.

Chûn Quoit

Disappointingly, this site was the least productive in terms of transpersonal dream content. The arduous nature of the site – high exposed moorland and cramped inside space – limited the number of people volunteering to sleep there. All the volunteers who did make it dreamt of animals, primarily dogs and horses, but jungle animals too – even ant-eaters! There were, however, no clear or noteworthy correspondences between dreams. Two dreamers did dream about rocks specifically, possibly due to the surrounding rock environment of the dolmen semi-lucidly influencing the sleeper:

PJ: Surfaces with [angular] marks ... Surfaces grey, the marks are white ... A grey rock-like surface, possibly the interior of the dolmen but with these marks. Whether the marks were symbols I really do not know.

CR: ...what looked like huge rocks. I looked at them and it was kind of a labyrinth and it looked like a rock I saw just two days ago at a fossil dealer's shop and then I realised that I was very small and wandering through that rock and that rock turned into a kind of cliff and I was kind of walking on that cliff but without my feet...

Figure 110. This volunteer is a cultural anthropologist who, in a single day, flew from Hamburg to the UK, then took the long train journey down to Cornwall, in order to sleep in Chûn Quoit that night. Here he poses with the dolmen around midnight before settling into the monument's cramped space perchance to have Stone Age dreams.

The dreamer PJ had a strong semi-lucid dream of going out of the dolmen and walking anti-clockwise around it. (Lucid dreams are ones where the dreamer awakes while still in a dream and remains physiologically asleep.)

Many dreams contained colours, the dominant recurring ones being grey, white and red. (The red may be due to the red flashlight used to periodically check the dreamer's eyes for REMs.)

Madron Well

There is only a limited amount of dream content material available for this site (i.e. the only digitised records available to me at this time are the ones which had both home and site dreams) – four dream volunteers only. I have grouped them here for simplicity. I have already described my own dream at this place, but what I looked for is any dream content that occurred here that does not appear in dreams at the other sites. Interestingly, even in this limited material two such motifs do appear – namely, strong references to patterns and flowers:

MJ: You know the pattern wet sand makes on the beach, how it is sort of bubbly? I don't know much else. Lots of strange patterns I don't know... sort of like cat claws. Almost like crescent moons but not exactly ... more like cat claws a lot fatter at one end sort of ... So many patterns ...

M-J (different REM period): It was ... there was something like the underside of a bathmat - how the suction cups are arranged, they looked like flowers, everything was perfectly regular.

TH-S: The field is a very strong image in this dream. I've been in a vehicle in this field. It was quite a lot to do with that. The field is quite large and there is a hay crop or something. Lots and lots of flowers, although growing in and around all this hay. Really lovely pinks and yellows with all these flowers...

Figure 111. A dream session taking place alongside the well/font in the ruined chapel.

These dreamers never met or communicated with one another. Other recurring dream content by these and the other volunteers at Madron involved water and animals (including a leopard with spots, so perhaps another pattern indicator). However, the recurring water imagery was probably prompted by environmental factors, namely the sound of the trickling water in the font, and a general reference to animals recurred at other sites too.

Carn Ingli

There is unfortunately little material to work on here. This is partially because there were few volunteer dreamers for this locale, due to the difficulty accessing it, high on an exposed rocky ridge, and also due to the vagaries of transcription not all the dream reports are available to me at the time of this writing.

Despite the paucity of dream content, there are a couple of faint hints of transpersonal dream imagery occurring that are unique to this site as compared to the other three dream locations.

Military references:

> **T H-S:** It's ... a stone structure that looks like a stone wall except that you realise that it's ... an army post. And there are soldiers on it and we're camped out. This army post is part of this set-up that's happening around us ... Around this army post ... these soldiers on it and it's swivelling. It's like a bridge. It's not really a bridge ... it's more a platform...

> **PH:** I'm dreaming about the list of people who are officers in... I don't know what it is... They all wear costumes of different centuries ... a list of all ... who these people are. That 's about it really.

Figure 112. A tent set up amidst the rocky crags of Carn Ingli in
preparation for a night's sleep/dream session.

(There have been long-time local rumours of the sounds of
disembodied marching feet and guttural voices being heard on
Carn Ingli.)

Monochrome references:

DD: There's men, women and children - black and white
children - and a man started by saying "This is Friday" and
it wasn't Friday. That's all.

ST: ...dreamt that we had a black and white TV set ... and
on it was a woman being interviewed by somebody ... she'd
just had been married and had been elevated to some sort
of royal position ...

But the especially interesting thing about the Carn Ingli sessions
was that most of the volunteers experienced some measure of
partial or full lucid dreaming. Sometimes this is alluded to in
dream reports – e.g. "It was really strange because it was ... just

one of those dreams ... that of doing exactly what you' re doing except weirder. It was exactly here except it was somehow more spacious. Somehow. It was on the top of a mountain, but there was more room around because there was all this grazing and all these animals, particularly reindeer". But at others, as can be heard on the tape recordings, the volunteer dreamer would argue with the helper that they had got up to urinate behind a rock while the helper assured them that had not happened. In one case the dreamer simply would not accept that he hadn't got up from the sleeping bag.

On one session, the helper explained that the tape was clear before the session started – they had tested it – but that in the background music somehow "got on" the tape as recording was taking place during a dream recall. Anomalous radio reception? Variations in tape speed also occurred – the helper speculated that this may be due to temperature changes. (It is worth remembering that this site has strong magnetic anomalies.)

Carn Euny

Because it was a relatively spacious and covered site, more dream content was collected here than at the other monuments (we didn't dictate to volunteers which site they chose to sleep in). Here are just a few snatches from just seven people's dream reports obtained at Carn Euny. The excerpts have been arranged so as to better highlight content similarities.

> **MS:** I dreamt that I was awake ... and these people turned up and they had this dog with them ... a beige dog. And there was a cat ...

AR: ...I turned off for the Carn Euny turning ... Something went across in front of the bull-bar on the jeep ... I assumed it was a cat. It was big and beige ...

MVB: ...a sense of processing ... of going from one place to another

AR: ... on this flat lane, walking with these people who were hikers or going somewhere ... a very friendly bunch of people ... Definitely the bustle of people going somewhere ...

BH: ... something to do with walking. It was sort of flattish sort of countryside ... I'm definitely walking around in this countryside ... I don't think I knew of any of these people ... It was a crowd of about five or six people ... we were walking around the area...

Figure 113. A volunteer preparing for a night's dreaming session inside the corbelled chamber.

DS: They're [the people] holding my hands ...I think they're going to take me somewhere ... It was all right though ... They were nice...

BH: There was quite a lot of people and it was something to do with food ...

AR: ...This person had set up selling ice creams and things...

MVB: ...A very tall chocolate cake ...

DS: I dreamt that we broke into a new tomb somewhere near here ... this enormous great carved ... with huge tusks and eyes, painted eyes ....

GH: ... little boy with an old face, deformed face, or something ... It was slightly nightmare-ish...

BH: ...stuck on the wall... was a big round thing and it had a face on it ... It wasn't really a human face ... It had big eyes, roundish eyes...

THS: ... I'm in the audience ... there's someone else who's just finishing an act. A singer or something...

BH: ... watching a show that was going on, sort of play thing but it was also something people sort of partook in ... we were sitting in the audience....

A general sense of elements of connected imagery and narrative is surely discernible across these Carn Euny examples: beige-coloured

Figure 114. A volunteer entering the Carn Euny fogou ahead
of settling down to a dream session there.

animals, people processing, flat terrain, a face or mask with painted
eyes, a performance of some kind, and even food/confectionery.
(The beige cats imagery, however, should probably be discounted
as this site was sometimes visited during sessions by two local farm
cats, one of which was beige in colour.) Keep bearing in mind that
these snatches from the dream records were recorded independently on-site on different occasions by volunteers with no connections
with one another. Could we be glimpsing some transpersonal,
site-associated information showing dimly through the distorting
glass of personal dream recall?

Whatever, it makes me realise the more dream material that
can be collected at a site, the more likely it becomes to be able
to detect some transpersonal threads of content. And looking
overall at this on-site dreaming effort, it would seem that a site
like Carn Euny that is conducive to sleeping is a better bet than
the more rugged sites that seem – in this embryonic experiment,
at least – to provoke lucid and semi-lucid dreaming.

If more extensive and rigorous work of this kind bears results that also suggest the accessing of site memory is possible, making these tentative results more scientifically credible, then a paradigm shift in our understanding about the nature of consciousness will have been signalled by this modest pilot study, and something approaching Durrell's intuition at the Greek dream temple sites will have been strengthened. If not, the exercise will at least have produced a unique body of dream reports that could provide a valuable database for future researchers.

7

NUMINOSITY AND SACRED PLACE

The deepest, strongest of the powers of ancient sacred places is numinosity. Ironically, it is the hardest one to describe. Here are a couple encyclopaedia attempts to define it:

"A strong religious or spiritual quality; indicating or suggesting the presence of a divinity."

"Arousing spiritual or religious emotion; mysterious or awe-inspiring."

Numinous is derived from the Latin *numen*, referring to a deity or spirit presiding over a thing or place. (It was C.G Jung who coined *numinosity* from it.) In the particular context of sacred places, especially but by no means exclusively natural ones, we might term it *genius loci*, the spirit of a place – its 'atmosphere'. It is felt, intuited, rather than perceived, even if it is prompted by a cast of light or atmospheric conditions.

The German philosopher and theologian Rudolf Otto popularised the word numinous in his 1917 book, *Das Heilige*, published in English as *The Idea of the Holy* in 1923. He considered feelings of eeriness or awe to be the earliest manifestation of the holy. This is how, in Otto's opinion, the concept of the 'holy place' developed:

The English "This place is haunted" shows a transition to a positive form of expression. Here we have the obscure basis of meaning and idea rising into greater clarity and beginning to make itself explicit as the notion ... of a transcendental Something, a real operative entity of a numinous kind, which later, as the development proceeds, assumes concrete form as a 'numen loci', a daemon, an 'El', a Baal, or the like.

In Genesis xxviii 17, Jacob says: "How dreadful is this place! This is none other than the house of Elohim". This verse is very instructive for the psychology of religion; it exemplifies the point that has just been made. The first sentence gives plainly the mental impression itself in all its immediacy, before reflection has permeated it, and before the meaning-content of the feeling itself has become clear or explicit. It connotes solely *primal numinous awe*, which has been undoubtedly sufficient in itself in many cases to mark out 'holy' or 'sacred' places, and make them spots of awful veneration ...

The German expression *Es spukt hier* (literally, it haunts here) is also instructive. It has properly no true subject, or at least it makes no assertion as to what the *es*, the 'it', is which 'haunts'; in itself it contains no suggestion of the concrete representations of 'ghost', 'phantom', 'spectre', or 'spirit', common to our popular mythology. Rather it is the statement of the pure expression of the emotion of eeriness or 'uncanniness' itself, when just on the point of detaching and disengaging from itself a first vaguely intimated idea of a numinous something, an entity from beyond the borders of 'natural' experience. (Otto 1917/1923)

Otto very accurately explained numinous as a "non-rational, non-sensory experience or feeling whose primary and immediate object is outside the self". Put another way, it could also be said that it is a sense that develops as an interaction between an individual's personal psychology and a place. In this view, the site, the place, has agency; such animistic thinking may be alien to modern ways of thought, but the most ancient of religious impulses was that of animism, in which natural phenomena and the land and all within it, animate or inanimate, were seen as being suffused with spiritual qualities, as being ensouled. The classical philosophers conceived of a world soul, *anima mundi*. Spirit of place can be seen as a microcosmic version of this. Plato said such an aspect of place could only be grasped by "dreaming with our eyes open" (Walter 1988). Scholar John E. Smith has noted that while the experience of the holy can intrude upon us "whether we will or not", we must go to a special place in order to realise its holiness (Smith 1992). In other words, we have to seek sacred place out. While numinous events can sometimes seemingly choose us, or, at least, are random events, he feels that sacred places have an arresting function in that they "lead us to respond in awe to the Holy".

Places that provoke numinous reaction within us have been called "thin places". This is well expressed in Mescalero Apache ideas about some of their sacred places which they consider possess or contain a supernatural power, *diyi'*. Such power places "occur at points of intersection between the physical and spiritual worlds" (Carmichael 1994). The sacred site is conceived of as a kind of mirror, the physical world being merely a reflection of the deeper and more real spiritual world. Transformations occur when people make spiritual journeys from one side of the mirror to the other. Numinous places are "liminal tucked between the mundane and spirit world; they are entry points into another consciousness"

(Crumley 1999). This 'thin' view of sacred place is particularly well exemplified in the Hindu concept of the *tirtha*. This word, applied to a whole category of holy pilgrimage places typically situated on rivers, means "a crossing place", a "ford". This is not only physically descriptive of many of these places, but is also metaphorical. Scholar Diana Eck points out that the term *tirtha*, coming from a Sanskrit verb meaning "to cross over", can also signify a path or a passage in a more general sense.

> The word . . . belongs to a whole family of Indo-European cognates which are the great words of passage and pilgrimage in the West: through, *durch* [German for through, by, carried], and trans, as prepositions, and all of the many passage words related to them, which in English alone include ... transition, transform, transport, and transcend. (Eck 1981)

An ancient concept of the primal, numinous nature of what becomes known or identified as 'sacred place' is therefore deeply embedded in Western languages.

Places become regarded as sacred for all kinds of cultural reasons, as we have noted elsewhere in these pages, but the first places sensed as holy, as numinous, were natural places. Thus, it was the Earth itself that provided the primary points of sanctity, so to speak, and all human groups started out by selecting certain natural places as special. Such locations were sometimes eventually embellished with rock engravings or paintings, or minimal pieces of architecture, and sometimes these developed into monumental structures or inspired monuments to be raised in their vicinity. The numinous impulse that may affect us inside an ancient church, a mosque, a temple or other developed, sophisti-

Figure 115. Sunbeams penetrate the ancient Mayan ritual cave of
Lol-tun, Yucatan.

Figure 116. The numinous quality of the massed and convoluted
stalactites inside the Dictaean Cave still inspire awe in the visitor
as they did the ancient Greeks, who left votive objects wedged
inside the calcite folds.

cated place of worship today found its first realisation in the caves, groves, mountains, gorges, rivers, springs, and other natural places that spoke of mystery and awe to our distant forebears.

Underlying it all, the natural ancient sacred places can still retain the power to affect us directly at psychological or numinous levels – even if we cannot now share the specifically cultural, religious ideas with which the ancients clothed that primal response at such locations. For instance, one may not now believe in the Greek pantheon, and to us Zeus may be diminished to a thunderstorm, but the Dictaean Cave in Crete, identified in myth as his birthplace, will nevertheless still trigger a reaction of awe in the modern visitor.

Even the places of worship belonging to the relatively new-fangled 'world religions' work best for us at the psycho-spiritual level when they emulate natural places. So Gothic cathedrals, for example, were designed to reproduce the sensation of being in a forest of tall trees – soaring space defined by trunk-like columns reaching to the roof, arching over like a forest canopy; a cool, dim place, with occasional gleams of light. Or, a mosque glitters and shines with the intricacy of natural forms and otherworld glamour – the garden of paradise.

Depending on the condition of person and place, the numinous can manifest as an uplifting experience, or a somewhat frightening one (awe-ful), or simply – if that is the word to use – a suffusion of poetic sensibility.

I can recall a few personal experiences of all these. During fieldwork on the Dragon Project, I visited the Rollright Stones on a great many occasions at all times of day or night, and in all seasons. Over time I became aware, as did other workers on the Project, that the stone circle evinced definite 'moods', whether it is animistic to say that or not. On one occasion, I had to check in with a volunteer monitor who was doing a 24-hour shift at the site. I arrived on my own at 11 o'clock at night, and discovered that there was nobody there. But on this evening, the stone circle, where I normally felt perfectly at ease, seemed exceedingly haunted and threatening. So much so, I felt profoundly uneasy and had to leave in a hurry. It later transpired that the volunteer monitor I had expected to see had also found the site to take on a different, "creepy" aura, and had fled in fear a few hours before I had arrived. On another occasion, I visited a prehistoric stone row in a remote part of Dartmoor. It was a gloriously sunny day and I was on my own. Over a few hours, I was happily conducting work at the site when I suddenly felt as if I was being watched. There were open and empty moorland views in all directions, and the sensation wasn't of being spied upon, but rather that it was the *site itself* watching me. (There I go, being animistic again.) Moreover, I felt unwelcome, as if my allotted time there had expired; I felt that I needed to leave in a hurry, so much so that I left a favourite hip-flask behind!

Figure 117. Stonehenge at night. Here illuminated, but in the quiet, unlit darkness it exudes a numinosity that isn't detectable in tourist-ridden daytime.

Other numinous moments have been less forbidding and cover a range of sensations. A major example was on Silbury Hill, as already described (Chapter 5). But I recall other examples. One is Stonehenge. I have always found the monument to be physically slightly underwhelming, not living up to the copious photographic images of it that flood television and magazines. But on one occasion I was there during night-time, and in the quiet darkness the stones took on an altogether more brooding and impressive quality than in daylight, seeming many times taller even than they actually are. The only way I can describe it is that the monument breathed a presence borne of deep time. A deep-rooted numinosity pervaded the place.

Or, again, I experienced a powerful sense of awe when visiting the ancient Mayan ritual cave of Balankanché near Chichen Itza in the Yucatan, Mexico. This was blocked for many centuries by a rock fall, and when archaeologists finally entered it they found votive pots and incense burners as they were left almost a thousand years ago. At the deepest point of the cavern system is a small cave in the centre of which is a fused stalactite-stalagmite looking remarkably like a stone tree (Fig. 118). Beyond, stretching away into unfathomable darkness is a subterranean lagoon. The combined effect of all these elements created a veritable psychic shock in me – that is the only way I can put it.

I had a beautifully uplifting experience the first time I visited Delphi, the ancient Greek oracle temple in its dramatic mountainside setting. It was shortly after a tremendous electrical storm, in which lightning appeared to flash horizontally through the deep ravine below the temple's location, as if old Zeus himself was out and about hurling his thunderbolts around. That build-up to my visit, and the scent released by the rain of the surrounding cypresses, combined to give me a powerful numinous experience.

Figure 118. The extraordinary fused stalactite-stalagmite 'tree' deep within the ancient Mayan ritual cave of Balankanché. It was clearly venerated as the Mayan World Tree, *Ya'ache Cab*.

Similarly, catching first site of fabled Glastonbury Tor, once an island, rising now in a curious, otherworldly way out of the Somerset Levels, has given me a fleeting numinous charge on several occasions. There are many further instances I could mention at many sacred sites, but in the final analysis, it is difficult to explain the precise nature of a numinous experience. It is something deeper than merely the pleasure of ruins or an enchanting natural place; it is the unique interaction between a person's psyche and the active, animistic agency of the place.

ANIMISM

A phrase like "animistic agency" perhaps requires a little more expansion. The idea of a given place having its own agency, its own ability to express or impose sacred power, is, I know, somewhat challenging for us today. In fact, animism is a huge, perhaps insurmountable, step for us in our culture to make – acquiring the understanding, the sense, that all elements of the non-human world are animate in some way, having conscious-ness of some kind at some level – rocks, rivers, soil, not to mention all the other-than-human entities (which includes not only plants and living organisms but also what are called 'spirits' in old parlance). It requires us to think outside our cultural box, even if only briefly, and shed received notions about the nature of reality and the nature of mind. Although animism is utter anath-ema to modern thought, it has been a way of knowing, a spiritual fact, to the countless ages of humanity that have preceded us.

Such mythopoetic relationship with the environment was one example of what the ethnologist Lucien Lévy-Bruhl called *participation mystique*. By this is meant a local relationship with the land that went beyond mere utility and subsistence. To the

Figure 119. Glastonbury Tor in moody lighting typical of the Somerset Levels. This prominent hill was once believed to be the entrance to Annwn, the Celtic Underworld, and the palace of the last Fairy king.

indigenous person, "Earth and sea are to him as living books in which the myths are inscribed" (Levy-Bruhl 1935). Another anthropologist, A. P. Elkin, put it more specifically when writing about indigenous Australasian peoples: "The bond between a person and his (or her) country is not merely geographical or fortuitous, but living and spiritual and sacred. His country ... is the symbol of, and gateway to, the great unseen world of heroes, ancestors, and life-giving powers which avail for man and nature". (cited in Lévy-Bruhl, p. 43)

In the West, this kind of relationship was noted at least as long ago as ancient Greece, where there were two words for subtly different senses of place, *chora* and *topos*. *Chora* is the older of the two terms, and was a holistic reference to place: place as expressive, place as a keeper of memory, imagination and mythic presence. *Topos*, on the other hand, signified place in much the way we think of it nowadays – simple location, and the objective, physical features of a locale. Topography. But, ultimately, even sacred places have nowadays become mere *topoi*.

Place-names can often survive through countless generations, providing echoes of the animistic relationship that existed in ancient landscapes. In Greenland, for instance, Inuit place-names include *Toornaarsutoq*, "the place with lots of spirits", and *Angakkussarfik*, "the place of the initiation of the shaman". In Celtic lands the word "pap", meaning female breast, was often applied to rounded hills and mountains, recalling a perception of an Earth Mother goddess residing in the very landscape that goes back deep into prehistory. In every land that had an indigenous language, place-names can provide clues to former sacred cartography.

Concepts of animism can take various forms. For many ancient societies the land was so alive it spoke to them in their dreams. A clear account of this was provided by a Paiute Indian, Hoavadunuki, who was a hundred years old by the time he was interviewed by ethnographers in the 1930s. The old Indian stated that a local peak, Birch Mountain, spoke to him in his dreams, urging him to become a 'doctor' (shaman). The old Paiute resisted, he said, because he didn't want the pressures and problems that would come with that (Steward 1934). Communication from this mountain occurred a number of times throughout the old man's long life and was not seen as strange or peculiar by him – indeed, the idea of the land being capable of speaking to humans was probably widespread in ancient sensibility.

Sacred soundscapes were simply a natural corollary of that sensibility. The basic notion of the land having speech, or of being read like a text, was lodged deeply in some schools of Japanese Buddhism – in early medieval Shingon Esoteric Buddhism, founded by Kūkai, for instance. He likened the natural landscape around

Figure 120. The Paps of Jura, seen from the closely adjacent island of Islay,
Scotland. Probably seen in prehistory as dramatic expressions of the Earth
Goddess, because a Neolithic stone row on Islay aligns to the peaks, and a
midsummer sunset alignment to the mountains is marked by a Neolithic site,
Ballochroy, on the Scottish mainland, 20 miles away.

Chuzenji temple and the lake at the foot of Mount Nantai, near
Nikko, to descriptions in the Buddhist scriptures of the Pure Land,
the habitation of the buddhas. Kūkai considered that the landscape
not only symbolised but was *of the same essence* as the mind of the
Buddha. Like the Buddha mind, the landscape spoke in a natural
language, offering supernatural discourse. "Thus, waves, pebbles,
winds, and birds were the elementary and unconscious performers
of the cosmic speech of buddhas and bodhisattvas," explains Allan
Grapard (1994).

This is reminiscent of the beliefs of the Kaluli and Umeda
people in Papua New Guinea. To them, birdsong emanating out
of the dense jungle foliage are, or were, the voices of the ancestors, that the living birds are giving voice to the spirits of the dead.
These peoples classified birds not by their plumage or appearance,
but by the songs they produce. Anthropologist Alfred Gell came
to realise that peoples like the Kaluli and Umeda who live in dense

forests tended to be acoustic cultures, and make hearing – and, in some cases, smell – the primary sense, ahead of vision. (The Kaluli even have a verb, *dabuma*, that melds the taking in of sensory information by ear or nose.) Gell observed that the Kalulis' spirit idea about birdsong was only one kind of "coding of acoustic experience": the sounds produced by rivers, streams, waterfalls and other environmental sounds enter the language of these New Guinea people by means of onomatopoeia. The Kaluli can "sing places" like waterfalls, navigating a sonic cartography. "Place, sound and social memory are fused together in Kaluli poetics," Gell wrote (1995).

It is only in our modern culture that, as a whole, we have stopped listening to the land within a spiritual context. If we could fashion a modern, suitably culturally-ingrained animistic model, it is clear we would treat the environment with much more respect.

Epilogue

Numinosity results from deep reflexes between mind and nature that we cannot properly articulate. It was the land, after all, that first taught us about sacred place – it was humankind's primal communion. It was the land and sky that endowed the places that originally became venerated with the various energies and moods of nature, and instilled the idea of the holy in our hearts and mind.

REFERENCES

Baker R., 1989. *Human Navigation and Magnetoreception*. Manchester: Manchester University Press.

Baring-Gould, S., 1900. *A Book of Dartmoor*. London: Methuen.

Barrett, J., 1994. *Fragments from Antiquity*. Oxford: Blackwell.

Bates, C. R., Bates, M., Gaffney, C., Gaffney, V., and Raub, T.D., 2019. "Geophysical Investigation of the Neolithic Calanais Landscape." *Remote Sensing* 11 (24). https://doi.org/10.3390/rs11242975

Berthier, F., 2000. *Reading Zen in the Rocks*. Chicago: University of Chicago Press. (Trans. G. Parkes)

Bevins, R.E., Ixer, R.A, Pearce, N.J.G., 2013. "Carn Goedog is the likely major source of Stonehenge doleritic bluestones: evidence based on compatible element geochemistry and Principal Component Analysis." *Journal of Archaeological Science* (42: February).

de Boer, J.Z., Hale, J.R., and Chanton, J., 2001. "New evidence for the geological origins of the ancient Delphic oracle (Greece)." *Geography*, (August).

Boivin, N., 2003/2004. "Rock Art and Rock Music: Petroglyphs of the South Indian Neolithic." Cambridge: *The McDonald Institute for Archaeological Research*. (And *Antiquity* (78), 2004).

Bord, J. and C., 1976. *The Secret Country*. London: Elek.

Boyd, C., 1998. "Pictographic evidence of peyotism in the Lower Pecos, Texas Archaic." *The Archaeology of Rock-Art* (C. Chippindale & P. Taçon, eds.). Cambridge: Cambridge University Press.

Bradley, R., 2000. *The Archaeology of Natural Places*. London & New York: Routledge.

Brennan, M., 1983. *The Stars and the Stones*. London: Thames & Hudson.

Brooker, C., 1983. "Magnetism and the Standing Stones." *New Scientist*, (13 January).

Brunton, P., 1935. *A Search in Secret Egypt*. London: Rider (and various other editions.)

Burl, A., 1985. *Megalithic Brittany*. London: Thames & Hudson.

Burl, A., 1987. "Moonwatch." *The Ley Hunter* (102).

Butler, S. and Purves, A. (eds.), 2013. *Synaesthesia and the Ancient Senses*. Durham: Acumen.

Carlson J.B., 1975. "Lodestone Compass: Chinese or Olmec Primacy? Multidisciplinary analysis of an Olmec hematite artifact from San Lorenzo, Veracruz, Mexico." *Science* (189: September 5).

Carmichael, D., 1994. "Places of Power: Mescalero Apache sacred sites and sensitive areas." *Sacred Sites, Sacred Places* (Carmichael, D., Hubert, J., Reeves, B., and Schanche, A. eds.). London: Routledge.

Clarke, D., and Roberts, A., 1990. *Phantoms of the Sky*. London: Hale.

Cook, I., 2003. *Ancient Acoustic Resonance Patterns Influence Regional Brain Activity*. Princeton: International Consciousness Research Laboratories (ICRL) Internal Report.

Cook, I., Pajot, S.K., and Leuchter, A.F., 2008. "Ancient Architectural Acoustic Resonance Patterns and Regional Brain Activity." *Time & Mind*, 1(1).

Crouch, D. P, 1993. *Water Management in Ancient Greek Cities*. Oxford: Oxford University Press.

Crumley, C. 1999. "Sacred Landscapes: Constructed and Conceptualized." *Archaeologies of Landscape* (Ashmore, W., and Knapp, A. eds.), Oxford: Blackwell.

Cunliffe, B., 1985. *The Roman Baths and Museum*. Bath: Bath Archaeological Trust.

Dams, L., 1984. "Preliminary findings at the 'Organ' sanctuary in the cave of Nerja, Malaga, Spain." *Oxford Journal of Archaeology* 3(1).

Dams, L., 1985. "Palaeolithic lithophones: descriptions and comparisons." *Oxford Journal of Archaeology* 4(1).

Darvill, T., 2006. *Stonehenge – The Biography of a Landscape*. Stroud: History Press.

David-Neel, A. 1932. *With Mystics and Magicians in Tibet*. New York: Claude Kendall. (Numerous other editions.)

Day, J. (ed.), 2013. *Making Senses of the Past*. Southern Illinois University Carbondale: Occasional Paper No. 40.

Dem, M., 1977. *Megaliths et Routes Secrets de l'Uranium*. Paris: Michel. (trans C. Rhone.)

Devereux, P. and York, A., 1975. "Portrait of a Fault Area". *Fortean Times* (then entitled *The News*) (8:11 & 12).

Devereux, P., 1982. *Earth Lights*. Wellingborough: Turnstone Press.

Devereux, P., 1989. *Earth Lights Revelation*. London: Blandford Press.

Devereux, P., 1990. *Places of Power*. London: Blandford Press.

Devereux, P., 1991. "Three-dimensional aspects of apparent relationships between natural and artificial features within the topography of the Avebury complex." *Antiquity* (65).

Devereux, P., 1992. *Symbolic Landscapes*. Glastonbury: Gothic Image.

Devereux, P., 2001. *Stone Age Soundtracks*. London: Vega.

Devereux, P., 2002. *Mysterious Ancient America*. London: Vega.

Devereux, P., 2010. *Sacred Geography*. London: Octopus.

Devereux, P. and Wozencroft, J., 2014. "Stone Age Eyes and Ears: A Visual and Acoustic Pilot Study of Carn Menyn and Environs, Preseli, Wales." *Time & Mind* 7 (1). http://dx.doi.org/10.1080/1751696X.2013.860278

Dowson, T. and Lewis-Williams, D., 1989. *Images of Power*. Johannesburg: Southern Book Publishers.

Dowson, T., 1992. *Rock Engravings of Southern Africa*. Johannesburg: Witwatersrand University Press.

Dowson, T. A., 1998. "Rain in Bushman Belief, Politics and History: The Rock-Art of Rain-Making in the South-Eastern Mountains, Southern Africa." *The Archaeology of Rock Art*. (Chippindale, C. and Tacon, P., eds.). Cambridge: Cambridge University Press.

DuBois, C., 1908. "The Religion of the Luiseño Indians of Southern California." *American Archaeology and Ethnology* 8(3).

Eck, D., 1981. "India's Tirthas: 'Crossings' in Sacred Geography." *History of Religions* 20(4).

Edwards, L., 1949. "The Welsh Temple of the Zodiac." *Research*.

Eitel, E.J., 1873/1973. *Feng Shui*. Cambridge: Cockaygne 1973 edition. (Originally published in 1873 as *The Rudiments of Natural Science in China*.)

Evans, B.J., 1977. "Magnetism and Archaeology: Magnetic Oxides in the First American Civlization." *Physica B+C* (86–88, Part 3: January–March).

Fagg, B., 1956. "The Discovery of Multiple Rock Gongs in Nigeria." *Man* (56: February).

Fagg, B., 1956b. "The rock gong complex to-day and in prehistoric times." *Journal of the Historical Society of Nigeria* 1(3).

Fagg, B.,1957. "Rock Gongs and Slides." *Man* 57(32).

Farrington, I., 2017. "Aspects of the sacred and kingship at the Inka palace of Qespiwanka." Time & Mind 10(3). https://doi.org/10.1080/1751696X.2017.1341244

Foley, L. E.; Gegear, R. J.; Reppert, S.M., 2011. "Human cryptochrome exhibits light-dependent magnetosensitivity." *Nature Communications* 2 (Article 356)

Fort, C., 1923. *New Lands*. New York: Boni & Liveright. (Numerous subsequent edns.)

Fox, K.M., 2018. "Mana, māna, ā mānā paha? Ho ʻailona ā Ho ʻike paha? (Mana, māna, or mānā? Sign, portent, revelation, knowing, or seeing?) What is this experience? Who gets to speak?" *Time & Mind (The Oceanic Concept of Mana, Special Issue)*. 11(4).

Gaddis, V.H., 1967. *Mysterious Fires and Lights*. New York: Dell.

Gaona, J.M., Rouleau, N., Caswell, J.M., Tessaro, L., Burke, R.C., and Schumacher, D.S., 2015. "Archaeoacoustic Investigation of a Prehistoric Cave Site: Frequency-Dependent Sound Amplification and Potential Relevance for Neurotheology." Poster at *Towards a Science of Consciousness:* Helsinki Conference.

Gatton, M., 2017. "The Eleusinian Projector: The hierophant's optical method of conjuring the goddess." *The Oxford Handbook of Light in Archaeology* (Papadopoulos, C. and Moyes H., eds.). Oxford: Oxford University Press. (Online)

George, M., 1995. "Dreams, Reality, and the Desire and Intent of Dreamers as Experienced by a Fieldworker." *Anthropology of Consciousness* 6(3).

George, M., 2018. "Experiencing mana as ancestral wind-work." *Time & Mind* 10.2.

Goodman, J., 1977. *Psychic Archaeology*. New York: Berkeley medallion.

Grant, J.S., 1984. *The Gaelic Vikings*. Edinburgh: James Thin.

Grapard, A., 1994. "Geosophia, Geognosis, and Geopiety: Orders of Significance in Japanese Representations of Space", in *Nowhere: Space, Time and Modernity* (Friedland, R. and Boden, D., eds.). Berkeley: University of California Press.

Grinsell, L.V., 1976. *Folklore of Prehistoric Sites in Britain*. Newton Abbott: David & Charles.

Hamilakis, Y., 2013. *Archaeology and the Senses*. Cambridge: Cambridge University Press.

Harte, J., 1986. *Cuckoo Pounds and Singing Barrows*. Dorchester: Dorset Natural History and Archaeology Society.

Hawkes, J., 1973. *A Guide to the Prehistoric and Roman Monuments in England and Wales*. London: Cardinal.

Hedges, K., 1993. "Places to see and places to hear: rock art features of the sacred landscape." *Time and space: dating and spatial considerations in rock art research* (Steinbring, J., Watchman, A., Faulstich P. and Taçon, P., eds.). Melbourne: Australian Rock Art Research Association Occasional Publication 8.

Howells, W., 1948. *The Heathens*. New York: Doubleday.

Huffman, T.N. and Earley, F.L., 2017. "Apishapa rock art and Great Basin shamanism: power, souls and pilgrims". *Time & Mind* 10(2).

Huffman, T.N. and Earley, F.L., 2019. "The Smell of Power: The Apishapa Pilgrimage Trail." *Time & Mind* 12(4).

Hultman, M., 2010. "The Known Yet Unknown Ringing Stones of Sweden." *Changing Pictures – Rock Art Traditions and Visions in Northern Europe* (Goldhahn, J., Fuglestvedt, I. and Jones, A., eds.). Oxford: Oxbow Books.

Hultman, M., 2014. "Soundscape Archaeology: Ringing Stone Research in Sweden." *Time & Mind* 7(1). http://dx.doi.org/10.1080/1751696X.2013.860259

Huxley, A., 1959. *The Doors of Perception* (1954) and *Heaven and Hell* (1956). Single volume edn. Harmondsworth: Penguin.

Ivanhoe, F., 1979. "Direct correlation of human skull vault thickness with geomagnetic intensity in some northern hemisphere populations." *Journal of Human Evolution* 8(4).

Ixer, R. A., 1996. "Ore Petrography and Archaeological Provenance." *Mineralogical Society Bulletin* 113.

Jahn, R.G., Devereux, P., and Ibison, M., 1996. "Acoustical resonances of assorted ancient structures." *Journal of the Acoustical Society of America* 99(2).

Jaynes, J., 1976. The Origins of Consciousness in the Breakdown of the Bicameral Mind. Boston: Houghton Mifflin.

Keepin, W., 1993. "Lifework of David Bohm. River of Truth." *Re-vision* 16(1) (Also online: http://www.vision.net.au/~apaterson/science/david_bohm.htm)

Kleinitz, C., 2003-4. Included in *The Central Amri to Kirbekan Survey: A Preliminary Report on Excavations and Survey* (Fuller, D.Q., ed.).

Krippner, S. and Ullman, M., 1973. *Dream Telepathy.* New York: Macmillan.

Krippner, S., Devereux, P. and Fish, A., 2003. "The Use of the Strauch Scale to Study Dream Reports from Sacred Sites in England and Wales." *Dreaming* 13(2).

Krippner, S, Devereux, P., Tartz, R., and Fish, A., 2007. "A Preliminary Study on English and Welsh "Sacred Sites" and Home Dream Reports." *Anthropology of Consciousness* 18(2).

Lambrick, G., 1983. *The Rollright Stones. The Archaeology and Folklore of the Stones and Their Surroundings: A Survey and Review.* Oxford: Oxford Archaeological Unit.

Laughlin, C., 2018. "Mana: psychic energy, spiritual power, and the experiencing brain." *Time & Mind* 10(2).

Lauhakangas, R., 1999. "A lithophonic drum in Lake Onega." *Adoranten* (Scandinavian Society for Prehistoric Art).

Levin, T., and Suzukei, V., 2006. *Where Rivers and Mountains Sing: Sound, Music and Nomadism in Tuva and Beyond.* Bloomington: Indiana University Press.

Lévy-Bruhl, L., 1935. *Primitive Mythology.* University of Queensland Press (1983 edn.)

Lewis-Williams, D., 2002. *A Cosmos in Stone.* Walnut Creek: Altamira Press.

Lewis-Williams, D. and Loubser, J.H., 2014. "Bridging Realms: Towards Ethnographically Informed Methods to Identify Religious and Artistic Practices in Different Settings." *Time and Mind* 7(4).

Liwosz, C., 2017. "Petroglyphs and *Puha*: how multisensory experiences evidence landscape agency." *Time & Mind* 10(2).

Loose, R.W., 2008. "Tse'Biinaholts'a Yalti (Curved Rock That Speaks)." *Time & Mind* 1(1).

Lund, C.S., 2019. "Ringing Stones in Sweden in the Past and Present." *Time and Mind* 12 (1).

Mac Manus, D., 1959/1973. *The Middle Kingdom.* Gerrard's Cross: Colin Smythe (1973 edn.).

Magin, U., 1987. "Highland Mysteries", *Info* 51.

Mattioli T., Farina, A., Armelloni, E., Hameau, P. and Diaz-Andreu, M., 2017. "Echoing landscapes: Echolocation and the placement of rock art in the Central Mediterranean." *Journal of Archaeological Science* 83.

Mattioli, T. and Diaz-Andreu, M., 2017b. "Hearing rock art landscapes: a survey of the acoustical perception in the Sierra de San Serván area in Extremadura, Spain." *Time & Mind* 10(1).

Mazel, A., 2011. "Time, Color, and Sound: Revisiting the Rock Art of Didima Gorge, South Africa." *Time & Mind* 4(3).

Menegat, R., 2019. "How Incas Used Geological Faults to Build Their Settlements." *Geological Society of America* 51(5). https://www.geosociety.org/GSA/News/pr/2019/19-38.aspx

Mereaux, P., 1981. *Carnac – une Porte vers l'Inconnu*. Paris: Laffont. (trans. C. Rhone)

Mertz, B., 1987. *Points of Cosmic Energy*. Saffron Walden: C.W. Daniel (English language edn.)

Morrison, T., 1987. *The Mystery of the Nazca Lines*. London: Nonesuch Press.

Mountford, C.P., 1968. *Winbaraku – and the Myth of Jarapiri*. Adelaide: Rigby.

Noyes, M.H., 2018. "The celestial roots of mana". *Time & Mind* 10(2).

Otto, R., 1924. *The Idea of the Holy*. Oxford: Oxford University Press.

Ouzman, S., 2001. "Seeing is deceiving: rock art and the non-visual." *World Archaeology* 33(2).

Pager, H., Mason, R.J. and Welbourne, R.G., 1971. *Ndedema*. Graz: Akademische Druck.

Pennick, N. and Devereux, P., 1989. *Lines on the Landscape*. London: Hale.

Persinger, M. and Schaut, G., 1988. "Geomagnetic factors in subjective telepathic, precognitive and post-mortem experiences." *Journal of the American Society for Psychic Research*, July.

Randles, J., 1983. *The Pennine UFO Mystery*. London: Granada

Rajnovich, G., 1994. *Reading Rock Art: Interpreting the Indian Rock Paintings of the Canadian Shield*. Toronto: Natural Heritage/ Natural History Inc.

Reznikoff, I., 1995. "On the sound dimension of prehistoric painted caves and rocks". *Musical Signification* (Taratsi, E., ed.). Berlin: Mouton de Gruyter.

Rifkin, R.F., 2009. "Engraved art and acoustic resonance: Exploring ritual and sound in North-Western South Africa." *Antiquity* 83(321). 10.1017/S0003598X00098859

Rodríguez-Pascua, M.A., Benavente Escobar, C., Rosell Guevara, L., Grützner, C., Audin, L., Walker, R., García, B., and Aguirre, E., 2019. "Did earthquakes strike Machu Picchu?". *Journal of Seismology* (October).

Saunders, N., 2003. "Technologies of Power and Enchantment in Pre-Columbian Goldworking." *Gold and Power in Ancient Costa Rica, Panama, and Columbia* (Quilter, J. and Hoops, J., eds.). Washington D.C.: Dumbarton Oaks.

Screeton, P., 1974. *Quicksilver Heritage*. Wellingborough: Thorsons.

Scullard, H.H., 1979. *Roman Britain*. London: Thames & Hudson.

Shallis, M., 1988. *The Electric Shock Book*. London: Souvenir Press.

Sheldrake, R., 1981. *A New Science of Life*. London: Blond and Briggs.

Skinner, S., 1982. *The Living Earth Manual of Feng Shui*. London: Routledge.

Smith, J. 1992. "The Experience of the Holy and the Idea of God." *Experience of the Sacred* (Twiss, S., and Conser, W., eds.). Providence RI: Brown University Press.

Steward, J., 1934. "Two Paiute autobiographies". *Publications in American Archaeology and Ethnology*. Berkeley: University of California.

Stewart, I. and Piccardi, L., 2017. "Seismic faults and sacred sanctuaries in Aegean antiquity." *Proceedings of the Geologists' Association*. 10.1016/j.pgeola.2017.07.009

Stewart, I. and Piccardi, L., and Farmaki, S., 2013. "*Map of Geomythology of Peloponnese*." PhD Dissertation, University of Patras.

Swentzell, R., 1985. *An Understated Sacredness*. Albuquerque: MASS: Journal of the School of Architecture and Planning, University of New Mexico, Fall.

Robert Tartz, R., Baker, R. and Krippner, S., 2006. "Cognitive Differences in Dream Content between English Males and Females Attending Dream Seminars Using Quantitative Content Analysis". *Imagination Cognition and Personality* 26(4).

Thomas, H. H., 1923. "The Source of the Stones of Stonehenge." *Antiquaries Journal* 3.

Thorpe, R. S., Williams-Thorpe, O., Jenkins, D.G., Watson, J.S., Ixer, R.A., Thomas, R.G., 1991. "The Geological Sources and Transport of the Bluestones of Stonehenge, Wiltshire, UK." *Proceedings of the Prehistoric Society* 57(2).

Tilley, C., 1994. *A phenomenology of landscape.* Oxford: Bloomsbury Academic.

Tributsch, H., 1982. *When the Snakes Awake.* Cambridge Mass.: MIT Press.

Ustinova, Y., 2009. "Cave Experiences and Ancient Greek Oracles." *Time & Mind* 2(3).

Waller, S., 1993. "Sound reflection as an explanation for the content and context of rock art". *Rock Art Research* 10(2).

Walter, E.V., 1988. *Placeways.* Chapel Hill: University of North Carolina Press.

Wang, C.X., Hilburn, I.A., Wu, D-A., Mizuhara, Y., Cousté, C.P., Abrahams, J.N., Bernstein, S.E., Matani, A., Shimojo, S., and Kirschvink, J.L., 2019. "Transduction of the Geomagnetic Field as Evidenced from alpha-Band Activity in the Human Brain". *eNeuro* 18 March. https://doi.org/10.1523/ENEURO.0483-18.2019.

Watson, A. and Keating, D., 1999. "Architecture and sound: an acoustic analysis of megalithic monuments in prehistoric Britain." *Antiquity* 73(280).

Watson, A. & Keating D., 2000. "The Architecture of Sound in Neolithic Orkney". *Neolithic Orkney in its European Context* (Ritchie, A., ed.). Cambridge: McDonald Institute Monographs.

Watson, A. and Scott, R., 2017. "Materialising Light, Making Worlds: Image projection within the megalithic passage tombs of Britain and Ireland". *The Oxford Handbook of Light in Archaeology* (Papadopoulos, C. and Moyes, H., eds.). Oxford: Oxford University Press. (Online)

Watson, L., 1974. *Supernature.* London: Coronet.

West, J.A., 1985. *The Traveller's Key to Ancient Egypt.* New York: Knopf.

Weatherhill, C. and Devereux, P., 1994. *Myths and Legends of Cornwall.* Ammanford: Sigma Leisure.

Whitley, D., 1996. *A Guide to Rock Art Sites: Southern California and Southern Nevada.* Missoula, Montana: Mountain Press.

Williams, W.J. and Stoddart, D.M, 1978. *Bath – Some Encounters with Science*. Clevedon: Kingsmead Press.

Zink, D., 1979. *The Ancient Stones Speak*. London: Paddington Press.

NOTE: Paul Devereux's Amazon author's page, which includes blog articles, photos, and further information, is at:
https://www.amazon.com/Paul-Devereux/e/B001HD1M42

ACKNOWLEDGEMENTS

If I were to try and cite all the people who have helped me over the years in researching and studying the various topics covered in this book, it would prove to be an invidious and impractical task. But as the Dragon Project figures to some degree here, I must mention especially all those volunteers who helped during its early phases, with fieldwork, monitoring work, on-site attendance, or the important but too often unsung 'behind-the-scenes' work, like transcriptions and data management. Though many have previously been acknowledged in my earlier publications, I would like to reiterate my collective appreciation here.

Regarding this particular book, the following have helped me by, variously, supplying relevant items of information, sharing their personal experiences, granting permissions, sharing fieldwork, providing inspiration, guidance, discussions, and more:

Dr. C. Richard Bates; Dr. Nicole Boivin; Dr. Caroline Boyd; Prof. Richard Bradley; Dr. David Clarke; Dr. Ian Cook; Roy Cooper; Lya Dams; Prof. Timothy Darvill; Brenda Dunne; F. L. Earley; Ian Farrington; Dr. Marianne 'Mimi' George; Dr. Joakim Goldhahn; Jeremy Hart; Ken Hedges; T.N. Huffington; the late Prof. Robert Jahn; Prof. Stanley Krippner; science historian David Kubrin; Prof. Charles Laughlin; Arnold Lettieri; the late Bill Lewis; Dr. Jannie Loubser; Dr. Aron Mazel; Alan Murdie; Dr. George Nash;

the late Prof. Michael Persinger; Andy Roberts; Sir and Lady Mark and Claire Rylance; John Steele; Erling Strand; Mark Turner; Dr. Aaron Watson; Dr. David Whitley; Jon Wozencroft; Jim Zintgraff, and also including those many others cited in the text.

(Apologies to anyone I've inadvertently left out – my memory is somewhat porous these days.) I am so grateful to them all.

Needless to say (but I'll say it), any errors herein are all mine.

My thanks also go to the peerless Greg Taylor of Daily Grail Publishing, without whom this book would never have seen the light of day.

And finally, my heartfelt gratitude, as ever, to my wife Charla and son Solomon, for braving numerous fieldwork sessions with me and always being prepared to help with technical and other essential 'backroom' work.

INDEX OF NAMES

CPSIA information can be obtained
at www.ICGtesting.com
Printed in the USA
LVHW102104130422
715979LV00011B/113

9 780645 209419